POLITICAL AND
ECONOMIC WRITINGS
OF A. R. ORAGE

A. R. ORAGE

POLITICAL AND
ECONOMIC WRITINGS

From *The New English Weekly* 1932-1934, with
a preliminary section from *The New Age* 1912

ARRANGED BY

MONTGOMERY BUTCHART

with the advice of Maurice Colbourne
Hilderic Cousens, Will Dyson, T. S. Eliot
Philip Mairet, A. Newsome, Maurice Reckitt
W. T. Symons

Essay Index Reprint Series

BOOKS FOR LIBRARIES PRESS, INC.
FREEPORT, NEW YORK

First Published 1936
Reprinted 1967

LIBRARY OF CONGRESS CATALOG NUMBER:
67-28762

PRINTED IN THE UNITED STATES OF AMERICA

FOREWORD

For nearly twenty years there thought and worked—it is in this case the same thing, for thought was his work—in the capital of England a man of unique quality, of whom not one in ten thousand Englishmen ever heard. He edited the most distinguished journal of his time. He sustained the integrity and kindled the imagination of many of its keenest spirits while they remained faithful, and bequeathed to them many of the fights with which they sought a wider, if not a more authentic fame. He found a new idea with which to challenge the slavery of his age, fostered it and gave it the power to do what it might avail to do against that slavery. It returned to him defeated, crushed by weapons the existence of which few had perceived, or even then conceived. He did not reproach his champion; he found another in a quarter where others disdained to seek him. Social Credit succeeded to the task of the Guild idea, and Orage retired to face more personal problems. His return was the signal for a welcome, the extent of which may have surprised him, but the practical results of which did not amount to much. The prophet was not wholly without honour, but he was still almost without disciples. Nevertheless the task began again; the incomparable style flashed out its illumination once more; the truth was not merely told but (how far more rare!) it was communicated. Yet even now only to the few; and it was with a surprised delight that one learnt he was to speak at last, via the B.B.C., directly to the thousands in whose cause he had spoken for twenty years,

7

The "talk" was given, and the champion of English liberties lay down that night to his earned repose.

I take Orage's discovery of, and welcome to, Social Credit to be not only the most decisive event in the history of that idea up till now, but one of the most striking examples of integrity and intelligence, acting hand in hand, which our day has witnessed. Orage in 1919 was past the age when men who have been leaders of thought, as he had been, willingly respond to the wrench of a new idea. Younger men, with less intellectual prestige or none, know the moral and mental effort it cost them to realign their sociological thinking to meet the challenge which Douglas demanded of them. Orage was ready for an instantaneous response, not only because nothing had been allowed to dull the keenness of his mind, but because no vested interests—of intellectual sectarianism any more than of financial gain— had been permitted to establish any greater claims than those of truth upon his spirit. His forward-looking intelligence, ahead as ever of its time, was already turned in the direction of the truth when it was revealed; he could recognize the discovery because he was ready for it. Such readiness is as rare as is the courage to accept the implications of it.

Orage, of course, was much more than a sociologist. Others can tell of the tremendous scope of his reading, of the clarity and illumination of his literary criticism, of that appetite for truth in its widest reach and its fullest strength which he sought in Theosophy, in Nietscheanism, in Psychology, and in that discipline at Fontainebleau which he so courageously accepted, sought—yet never, I think, satisfied himself that he had found; inevitably, as I believe, since there was one direction in which he did not look. Others will write of all this; but as a last salute of gratitude I will echo some words of one of my own friends who, being asked where he had been educated, replied: "I was educated in the 'New Age'." So in a measure was I, and if the acknowledgment is of a debt that will never be repaid, it is equally a tribute that would not, I think, have been rejected.

MAURICE B. RECKITT.

Editorial Note

The Editorial Committee whose names appear upon the title page have selected the extracts from the "Notes of the Week" of *The New English Weekly*, but for the selection of the extracts from *The New Age* and for the arrangement of the whole volume the responsibility is solely mine.

The extracts from *The New Age* were chosen not because feminism was a characteristic subject of Orage's writings, but because in these particular Notes we find an admirably clear, concise statement of Orage's political and economic theories (which centered then about the Guild Socialist idea) as they were before the discovery of Douglas and Social Credit, and because they convey a strong impression of the sustained clarity and vigour of his judgments upon current events. In his discussion of the very topical subject of feminism Orage condensed his views of the political and economic worlds, though the passage cannot convey an adequate impression of the depth and breadth of his influence during those years, nor of the vast range of the subjects upon which he exercised his judgment. For these impressions the reader is directed to Mr. Philip Mairet's volume, *A. R. Orage: A Memoir*. Orage's writings of this period must be collected and published later in a separate volume. The purpose of this one is to epitomize the political and economic views of Orage in the latest phase of his long development.

My attempt in arranging the passages from *The New English Weekly* has been not so much to provide a chronological record of Orage's comment upon current affairs from 1932 to 1934 as to find within that comment the universal principles which will assist the reader to discover the significant in his own and the world's affairs. The reader may, however, by reference to the appended table, transpose the ideational arrangement into the chronological. The Roman and Arabic numbers following the extracts refer respectively to volume and issue numbers.

Volume I	April 21st, 1932—October 13th, 1932
II	October 20th, 1932—April 13th, 1933
III	April 20th, 1933—October 12th, 1933
IV	October 19th, 1933—April 12th, 1934
V	April 19th, 1934—October 11th, 1934
VI	October 18th, 1934—November 8th, 1934

MONTGOMERY BUTCHART

CONTENTS

THE NEW AGE

THE NEW AGE

August 22 and 29, 1912

Of all the preposterous notions that could enter the heads
of women struggling for sex-emancipation the notion that
their struggle is comparable to the struggle of wage-slaves
for economic emancipation is the most absurd. We do not
say for one moment that the women's cause, whatever it
may be, is less important to the world at large than the cause
of labour. It may be, or it may not be. It is not even necessary
or legitimate, in our view, to compare the two causes. We
should as soon think of comparing the movement of men to
become supermen (if there is such a movement) with the
economic movement as the economic movement with the
movement for the emancipation of women as women. It is
quite enough, in our judgment, to name the two movements
in the same breath and to examine them as contemporaries
without concluding that their motives, or means, or ends,
are identical. Nevertheless, as we know very well, the two
movements have not only been compared, but practically
identified with each other. The suffrage-movement on the
one side has in its vocabulary, in its general public appeal,
and above all, in its actions, insinuated itself into the Labour

B

movement and persuaded the latter to accept it as a genuine economic and political ally. And the Labour movement (or rather its leaders) on the other side has not been backward in accepting the women's overtures. But it is obvious at the merest glance that the two movements have actually nothing in common save the vocabulary, the identity of which is easily explained by the origin of the pioneers of the militant suffrage movement. When it is remembered that Mrs. Pankhurst and her daughters, as well as Mr. and Mrs. Pethick Lawrence, were members of the Labour movement before they were Suffragists, their abilitude in the Labour vocabulary is natural. We have, however, to remark that either they did not understand the meaning of the economic terms when they were in the Labour movement, or, like the present Labour leaders, they, being Suffragists, do not understand them now. For one thing is quite certain, that the emancipation of women (we will explain our view of it in a minute or two) has nothing essential in common with the emancipation of labour. It is by misunderstanding that the confusion on both sides has arisen; and it is by mutual misunderstanding that the two movements continue, in spite of reason and events, to imagine themselves to be on parallel lines.

Whatever may be the difficulties, perhaps impossibilities, of the movement for the emancipation of labour from wage-slavery, nobody can deny either that the object is quite specific or that the wage-slaves desire it to a man and would actually be happier emancipated than bound. Nor is there anything either in nature or in racial habit (which is much the same thing) to say nay to the attempt or to the success of the attempt. On the contrary, nothing is more clear, more definite, and more concrete than the precise meaning and value attached to the terms, both of what may be called the theory of economic emancipation, and of the plan for carrying it out; and nothing is more certain than that every wage-slave has only to grasp the idea to call it his own. At the risk of a digression, the place of which is properly another issue of *The New Age*, we may remind our readers of the theory and plan of campaign we have recently been laying down in these pages. Every wage-slave, we contend, naturally desires to become economically independent of an employer—not of a master, be it observed, in his own trade, but of a profiteering employer. To free wage-slaves from the competitive wage-system and to emancipate them from the category of raw material in industry are, we say, the common and accepted conceptions of the meaning of Labour emancipation. The means, the obstacles and the subsequent emancipation are no less clearly realized—we do not say articulately by the rank and file of the Labour movement or instinctively by their present leaders, but, at any rate, by the Labour thinkers, whose leadership is only momentarily delayed. The means, it is now well understood, are mainly economic; the enemy is the capitalist; and the system which will supersede wage-slavery—if we succeed in abolishing wage-slavery—is Guild-Socialism or an active partnership, for industrial purposes only, between the State and the workers' unions.

We may contrast this definite and fully conscious movement for economic emancipation with the movement for emancipation among women as a sex. We challenge any of the women's leaders or thinkers to define in intelligible language the particular system or grievance, as distinct from men's, from which they desire to be emancipated. As wage-slaves, some of them, the women engaged in industry naturally desire to be free economically exactly as the men wage-slaves desire to be free. (At least, we will assume so for the moment.) But in wage-slavery, as in Heaven, there is no distinction of sex. In so far as women are wage-slaves in the industrial system their cause and the cause of men are one and the same. Everything, in fact, we have said of men wage-slaves applies to women wage-slaves in an equal degree. Get economic power, we say, by combination, by establishing a monopoly of your labour and by exerting your collective strength, and all the rest will follow. But it is plain that the wage-earners among women are not really the dominant factor in the women's movement for emancipation. Had that been the case, Mrs. Pankhurst and her daughters would never have left the Labour movement; nor would the wives of capitalists have joined in the movement for the emancipation of women. We do not see capitalists joining with Labour—why should capitalists' wives join with Labour's wives in a movement that is also economic? But if the object of women's emancipation is not economic, what, we ask, is it? What common object unites Lady Cowdray with Miss Annie Kenny that at the same time fails to unite Lord Cowdray with Miss Kenny's brother now editing the *Daily Herald*? We shall return later to this question, but for the moment we are engaged in proving that whatever the common object of Lady Cowdray and Miss Annie Kenny may be, that common object is not economic. In consequence of this, we really do not see any excuse for the Labour Party, at any rate, supporting the women's movement *on economic grounds*.

But before passing on to consider the second fallacy in the suffrage propaganda, let us clearly realize that not only is the women's movement not economic in the sense that the men employ the term, but it cannot be. We have allowed a paragraph or two back that women wage-slaves may naturally

be expected to desire the same kind of economic emancipation that men wage-slaves desire, and in so far as they do this
their cause is identical with that of Labour in general. But
there is every ground for doubting whether this is really the
case. Olive Schreiner has recently claimed all labour for
women's province equally with men. But her claim and
women's claim as represented by what they do are two
totally different things. Women, we may say, so far from
taking all labour for their province are in industry—to the
extent that they *are* in—under protest and against their will.
Not only is their demand for economic emancipation feeble
in comparison with that of men, but it is not nearly so strong
as their demand, made in a thousand feminine ways, to be
emancipated from the industrial system altogether. We are
not, as our readers will observe, bringing forward this statement as an accusation of women. Their instinctive prejudices
on the subject are probably wiser and more beneficent than
Olive Schreiner's. But the fact must be contrasted and not
merely compared with the corresponding fact in man,
namely, that industry is his very invention and the whole
system of it is his own contrivance. It follows, therefore,
that while a man finds himself at home in industry, loves it
for its own sake (organization apart) and desires nothing
better than to be engaged as a master in it, women feel themselves in industry to be not at home, they certainly do not
love it, and there is no honour in their eyes to be in it. Of
this last fact, surely the escape from industry into marriage
which many women make and most women would gladly
seize is sufficient proof. There are few women in industry
today who would not be married if they had the chance;
and married, for preference, to a man who could afford to
keep them out of industry for ever. With this kind of economic devotion in their hearts, it is improbable, we say

again, that the women's movement can be economic in character.

But with this misunderstanding and confusion of the real object of women's emancipatory movement has gone a corresponding misunderstanding of the means to be employed. As nobody has been allowed to forget, the means on which the women profess to rely exclusively are political means. They desire the Parliamentary vote. But for neither of the two purposes for which they conceive their movement to exist is either the vote or political action generally of the smallest conceivable value. For the spiritual object of the women's movement—the emancipation of women as women—the vote is plainly of no value. A Parliament composed entirely of women could not affect the relative natural characteristics of the male and female nature. God Himself, we are told, created man, male and female created He them; and what God has willed Parliament certainly cannot unwill. As well imagine, as we have suggested, that Parliament could make supermen of men as conceive that Parliament can raise the spiritual and psychological, the social and the physiological status of women as women. Whatever the means to this elevation of the type woman in the natural order may be, they are certainly not political; and the concentration on the political means is another proof of the profound misunderstanding of itself that the women's movement entertains. And as for its economic intentions—if it really possesses any—it is significant that the demand for political power as a means to economic power has arisen in women precisely at the moment when the economic movement of men wage-slaves has shown signs of dropping political action altogether. For the first time in the history of Labour, men are now in the position to estimate the value to them of the political

vote, and they have estimated that its value is very small indeed. Against economic forces the only force that is likely
to prove effective is economic force; for our experience of
Parliamentary power is that, with all the will in the world,
it cannot raise wages by a single penny. What warrant is
there for supposing that, if women's votes were added to
men's, the effect on economics would be any the greater?
So long as a small class possesses a monopoly of the main
instruments of production, so long, whatever Parliament
may say, will they command the economic situation.

Lastly, it argues a serious defect in instinct for women to
imagine that they can obtain by force what they fail to obtain by any other means. They simply cannot. It is conceivable that, as a result of their intellectual improvement, or as a
result of their spiritual development, women may one day
command enough respect of men to have the vote, or its
equivalent, thrust upon them. But it is not conceivable that
they can obtain the vote from unwilling men by *force
majeure*. In the first place, in actual force of every description
men are obviously superior to women. To assert this is not
to institute moral comparisons between the two sexes, but
simply to state an undeniable fact. If the decision of the
extension of the franchise to women is carried to the arbitra-
ment of force, there is not the smallest doubt of the result.
That particular Cæsar's verdict is a foregone conclusion. The
women may say, if they please, that they have not even yet
employed all the weapons of force in their armoury; behind
the hammer lies the revolver, and behind the revolver lies
the bomb. Be it so. But these weapons, even if the women
are demented enough to use them, will prove as powerless
as stones and hammers. The Russian revolutionaries have
certainly been more militant than the women in England

can possibly be; yet what has been the result of their methods of violence? Both the economic and the political constitutions of Russia remain pretty much what they were before a single bomb was exploded. Until, we say, the men of England consent of their own free motion to extend the franchise to women, the conquest of the franchise by the militants is a hopeless endeavour. And not to have realized this argues, in our opinion, a derangement of instincts in the militant women. But not less fallacious is the belief that irritation and importunity will accomplish what reason and persuasion have not done and what force alone cannot do. It is intensely annoying, but it is no more, when militant women interrupt public and private meetings, waylay Ministers, and create stairhead scenes in the public streets. Annoying and worrying, we say, but no more. Men's minds will not be changed by merely being nagged and ragged on a subject already decided by them. On the contrary, their self-respect demands that they should maintain their attitude even at the cost of suffering a little martyrdom for it. Individual men, here and there, may yield to feminine importunity; a percentage of homes have been ruined, indeed, by this weakness; but men in the mass have not only no intention of yielding, but they would cease to be men if they did. The conclusion is that neither by force nor by besetting can women obtain the vote; and their militant methods, in consequence, are a profound mistake.

The existence of three such fallacies as we have examined in full blast in the women's movement amply explains, we contend, the failure of the movement to make any progress. But worse even than making no progress at all is to produce a reaction or a progress in the direction contrary to our desire. We are strongly inclined to believe that, far from

having advanced the women's cause, spiritually or economically, the women's movement, under the direction of Mrs.
Pankhurst and her daughters, and of Mr. and Mrs. Pethick
Lawrence, has actually militated against it. Our evidence,
we admit, is not susceptible of production in a court of
reason; but in a court of taste it would, we think, be decisive.
Let any of our readers, women as well as men, weigh in their
minds their judgment of the value of the women's movement today against their judgment of its value three or four
years ago. And let them then apply the result to their honest
estimate of women's status today as compared with women's
status a few years ago. There can, we believe, be no doubt
what the conclusion must be if the values so compared are
fairly discerned and estimated: women as a sex have lost
ground. Three or four years ago there was in the public
mind in regard to women an expectation and a hope of
which the literature of the day was only a pale reflection.
Ibsen's dictum that the future was to workmen and women
had undoubtedly seized the imagination of England no less
than that of Continental Europe. The public anticipated
something both of workmen and women. What exactly
that something was, the public, of course, could not divine;
but it was to be of the nature of a happy surprise for humanity and the initiation of a new order of society. We are not
examining now the issue of the workmen's movement for
giving the world this happy surprise; but in the case of the
women's movement we may say, without fear of causing
Ibsen to rise from his grave to contradict us, that the world
has been bitterly disappointed. All our romantic expectations
of what women were about to do have been transformed
into dull confirmations of the world's previous judgment
that women can do nothing in particular that men cannot do
better. And this fresh disillusion, we maintain, is a positive

loss to women, both in regard to their estimate of themselves and in regard to the public estimate of them. If indeed, it has, as we believe, been brought about by the militant women's movement, the women of England and the world have little to be grateful for to the founders and conductors of the W.S.P.U.

We said we have no evidence for this that we could produce in a court of reason; but there are facts enough for an act of judgment if our readers desire to make it. It was obvious from the outset that, if the women were to improve their position relatively to men, they would have to do so by improving the status, opportunities and rewards of marriage, or by improving their economic position in national industry. For women who are not economically independent, in fact, there is only the choice between marriage, licit and illicit, and industry; and into one or other of these occupations the majority of women must certainly go. Of the two occupations, however, there is not the least doubt in our mind that one is a vocation and the other a second-string occupation in the majority of cases—occupation, moreover, in which women are distinctly inferior to men. Thus it follows that the reform of marriage takes precedence in importance over the reform of the economic conditions of unmarried women, and should have been advocated in preference to the latter. But, examining the facts as they stand at this moment, we see that not only has the economic position of women in industry remained the same—they, like the men, are wage-slaves, and their wages are fixed competitively, and therefore lower even than men's—but what may be called without offence the marriage market has dwindled in its demands. Just at the very moment that the women are engaged in making extravagant demands, the effective demand for their services, either as wives or as wage-slaves, is going down. But on a falling market of this character it is quite impossible to raise status by ordinary means. Extraordinary means might conceivably have been employed. If, for example, some hundreds of thousands of women had become nuns devoted to asceticism and charity, the economic as well as the spiritual effect would have been considerable. But as it was, and with ordinary means, they added to the impediments of their marriage by their new demands, and at the same time depressed the economic market for men by competing practically as blacklegs in industry. We do not know if it is realized that of the twenty million adults of our population only seven millions are married. With the tightening up of capitalism, this number will inevitably become less. How is it possible for women to raise their status while they are being driven more and more from marriage and more and more into the lower branches of industry?

Along with this evidence of declining status, however, we may name other symptoms, concomitants if not consequences of the fallacies in the women's movement. We have already mentioned the ex-orientation of instincts revealed by women in their mistaken choice of means and ends in their propaganda. This is a serious matter, both from their own and from society's point of view. The assumption we may make is that Nature, when it created a world of differentiated sex, did so in response to specific needs and in adaptation to specific, if only instinctive, intentions. From this somewhat theological point of view, the economy of human society demands that of this differentiation the best, and not the worst, should be made; and the best can only be made of it if the differentiation is frankly recognized and steadily perfected. In other words, the good of the race will best be served if men become more manly and women more womanly. This is, perhaps, a hard doctrine for women who have fed on the dangerous doctrines of Ibsen and Shaw; but the proof of its truth lies simply in its demonstration by experience. Good for society or the race, or not, the fact remains that women, as they become more womanly, become more pleasing and profitable to themselves. On the other hand, as they approximate to what they think is emancipation, they become discontented with themselves and the world, and profitless to both in the same degree. Discontent with a decree of nature, in fact, is the predominant emotion of the women's movement. At bottom they are revolting, not from man or from social organization, but from nature itself; and since such a revolt can only arise when, from some cause or other, the instincts have lost their unity and have become anarchic, the conclusion is that, before even the women's movement was begun, the seeds of its subsequent fallacies and failure had been sown in women's minds. But if women's instincts have become anarchic, the instincts of men have shown signs, under the influence of the women's movement, of following suit. We have had constantly for some years to deplore the spread of sentimentality in men, of a sentimentality that can only be regarded as effeminacy. We have no doubt whatever of the cause to which we must attribute this. It takes women to make men; and while in our society women as women are losing their instincts, the effect on men at large is similarly disastrous. The effeminate male suffragist we can only regard as the counterpart and the product of the militant female suffragist, and both alike are symptoms of a declining type. There is no value to be derived, either by themselves or society, from either of these allied species, and the sooner both of them become extinct the better it will be for everybody. No wife, certainly, whose husband can remain a man long remains a suffragist; and we commend this axiom to our readers' attention as both a destructive and a constructive criticism of the women's movement.

But enough for the present of the errors of the movement that is now nearly dead. What of the true idea with which it started, but which has been buried under mountains of misconception? We have already hinted that the mystical idea of the emancipation of woman is not unlike the mystical idea of the transfiguration of man into superman. In both instances there is a conquest not by suppression but by illumination of the sex nature which humanity shares with the animals. In both instances, again, the conversion is interior, psychological and a matter of art rather than of reason. Finally, for the present, in both instances the conversion is towards a more complete and perfect naturalness, towards a state which all the illuminated instincts declare to be their goal. Setting aside, however, this aspect of the subject for which few are prepared, there is on a more intelligible plane of discussion an object for women's endeavour which may be rationally stated. Let us distinguish between Social Reform and Social Culture; and let us agree that the former is a purely economic and political work and the latter a work for voluntary groups of individuals. In the matter of Social Reform it is plain, we hope, that the whole problem concerns industry and industry only; its organization, its materials and the distribution of its products. Parliament, we have said, in so far as it summarizes and represents the industrial condition of England is merely the index of this. But it follows that for women, whose share in industry is small in comparison with that of men, Social Reform, while of immense indirect consequence, is of no direct consequence. Only to the extent of their industrial importance have they or can they have any influence on the organization of industry at all. Votes or no votes, their political pull is proportioned to their economic pull, and this latter being negligible their political power in any case would be negligible too. In Social Reform, therefore, their wisest course is to stimulate men to get through with it; not to attempt to do it themselves; for of all the impediments to Social Reform a Social Reforming woman, male or female, is the greatest. But in Social Culture both now and still more when Social Reform has been completed, their province is simply immeasurable. Even as it is and without any vote at all (nay, while their taste in general is execrable) their opinions in affairs of manners, fashions, the theatre, the social conventions, and a score of other aspects of social life, are decisive. How much wiser it would be of them, and how much more in accord with their natural genius and instincts, if instead of attempting to be better men in industry than Adam they were ambitious enough to attempt to become better women than Eve! Not only would men become more manly as women became more womanly, but society as a whole would breathe more happily from the presence in it of men and women each astride of their instincts and aiming at perfection in them.

We will not conclude these Notes without writing responsibly (that is, as if we were in imminent peril of being called upon to carry out our ideas) of the means that have been and that ought to be adopted for putting an end to the movement in so far as it is a movement of fallacies. It is obvious, we fear, that a mere demonstration of the unprincipled, irrational and anti-natural character of the women's movement is not sufficient to kill it. Such demonstrations may kill it for the women who dare listen to reason; but they can have no effect on the women who either dare not listen to reason or who cannot comprehend reasoning. As these latter classes have been in exclusive control of the militant section, it is useless, as we say, to hope that demonstration will put an end to the movement. On the other hand, the supplies on which the militants depend are largely in the hands of women who are not yet actively militant themselves and who may therefore be said to be not entirely lost to reason. For these, indeed, reasoning should be continued and preferably by people whose opinions carry weight. Sir Almroth Wright's letter, for example, in *The Times* was a terrific anti-suffrage thunderbolt. Such men should be encouraged by the Cabinet to continue that type of enlightenment. But there remains the problem of what should be done with the women who make a public nuisance of themselves and even, in some instances, a public danger. Of all the methods to employ against them certainly the methods employed by the Government have been the worst conceivable, the least intelligent and the most ineffective. If the militant movement is killed, the credit of ending it will assuredly not lie with the Liberal Government. On the contrary, to the extent of their ability they have by confusion of mind connived at and, in a way, encouraged militancy from its earliest to its latest phases. And they have done this by the simple method of treating militancy as a crime instead of as a nervous disorder. Time was, we know, when lunatics were chained to walls like dogs, and witches were burned for sin. It did not reduce, we gather, either the tribe of the feeble-minded or the tribe of the psychic. Similarly, we may certainly affirm that the treatment of suffragist militancy as a criminal offence under any circumstances not only does not allay the nervous trouble, but flatters it into an aggravated

form. Our militants, on the whole, become more militant
with each successive dose of McKennaism and, what is even
worse, attract more sympathy as the doses are increased. We
say at once that no Home Secretary of Mr. McKenna's
proved poverty of ideas is capable of handling the militancy
movement as it should be handled. A medical statesman
might do it or even a philosopher with a sense of humour
might manage it; but a raw Philistine and "an Eton boy
grown heavy" is plainly the last person for a task requiring
both statesmanship and psychological finesse.

The actual facts of the situation are simple enough. In the
first place, there is no criminal intention among the militant
women even when, as a spoiled child may, they attempt to
fire theatres, burn houses and break windows. These things
are disagreeable to the sufferers, but they are, we are convinced, quite as disagreeable to the agents. To regard their
agents as responsible and deliberate criminals is to magnify
their state of mind and to distort it as well. Under no circumstances, we suggest, should militants for any pseudo-criminal
offence be sent to prison or made to pay a fine or, in fact,
treated as if they were what they were not. On the contrary,
they should be treated as what they are—namely, women
suffering from nervous disorder whose actions are temporarily beyond their normal control. What is, then, the treatment this fact dictates? Sentence to residence in a sana-
torium, a private hydro, a home of rest, or abroad for a
holiday under medical advice. Simply that and nothing
more. And, in the second place, it should be recalled that the
number of active militants is really small. There are not, we
calculate, more than about a hundred; and this number
would certainly be reduced if the first batch were deprived
of the martyrdom of prison and given the martyrdom of an

enforced holiday. For the militescent women now on the verge, perhaps, of militancy, a means of restraint has already been mentioned in these columns. The proper police for women are women. The Duke of Abercorn has organized a body of industrial bashi-bazouks for industrial order. Let some anti-suffrage society organize a similar body of women to keep suffragists in order.

August 22, 1912.

If we are fortunate enough to make our ideas as clear in these Notes as they are in our mind, the truth of several important conclusions in regard to the women's movement will emerge. First, we intend to show that the women's movement, though different from and opposed to the Labour movement, owes its origin to the same cause, namely, capitalism. Secondly, we shall prove that the remedies for their grievances specified by the women themselves and by their male champions, e.g. Mr. Shaw and Mr. Wells, would, if adopted, worsen and not better the condition both of women and of men. Thirdly, we hope to prove that the remedy, now well known, for the Labour grievance includes and is the true remedy for the women's grievance as well.

Without entering at this moment into a long exposition of the nature of capitalism, we may say that its well-known characteristics are three: production for profit instead of use, the private ownership of two of the means of production, and the treatment of the third means, namely, Labour, as a raw material simply. But it follows from this assumption of labour as a raw material, that labourers of whatever sex, age, or qualifications—so they be economically dependent and excluded from the possession of land or capital—may be and

c

will certainly be treated like all the rest of the raw materials of industry. That is, a constant endeavour will be made by capitalism to cheapen the cost in production of the raw material of labour by the same means as are employed to cheapen other raw materials. By reducing the actual cost of production, by enlarging the area of supply, and by economy in their use, most of the inanimate raw materials of industry have actually been enormously cheapened within each twelvemonth almost of the last fifty years. The cost of rubber as a raw material in industry, for example, has been remarkably reduced within the last few years by the addition of plantations to wild forests, by transplantation of rubber from India to South America, Burmah, and elsewhere, and by the admixture with pure rubber of various cheap amalgams for various purposes. The same is true of cotton. The same is true of cattle. And it stands to reason, reflection and experience that the same, *mutatis mutandis*, is true of the raw material of labour.

In its attempts, however, to cheapen the cost in industry of the raw material of labour capitalism has been met by certain difficulties peculiar, more or less, to the human race. These were of a kind which in one aspect were natural to man and therefore ineradicable, and in another were the outcome of long ages of habit. For example, it is natural to man to require a minimum amount of sleep, food, leisure and recreation; in this respect the demands of men differ only in degree from the demands of horses and other live stock. But in addition to these demands, involving a certain minimum cost of production and maintenance, man has the distinction over horses of being socially disposed, and of having acquired from this disposition certain habits of association which have been expressed in what we may call the great

human institutions. Of these we may name the institution of
castes and classes, the institution of local and national groups
of government, the institution of associations of kindred
workmen in guilds, and, lastly, the institution of marriage
and the family system. All these immemorial groupings of
human beings, however, were from the standpoint of capitalism so many obstacles to the free competitive circulation
of the raw material of labour. In other words, they militated
against the cheapening of labour in production which it was
one of the objects of capitalism to bring about. A taboo, for
example, instituted by one class for its own members against
certain forms of industry was obviously a sort of wall against
capitalism in that particular area. Again, the local and national bonds which had grown up militated against the
famous mobility of labour which was as necessary to capitalism as the mobility of cotton. The guild system, likewise,
was a perpetual obstacle to the cheapness of labour by reason
of its resistance to the spirit of competition. And, finally,
marriage and the family system had these disadvantages for
capitalism: that though undoubtedly the supply of labour
was maintained by these means, the cost was greater than it
need be for several reasons. First, the married man required
wages sufficient to keep not only himself, but a wife who
might or might not bear children to capitalism. Secondly,
women as a sex were exempted by privilege from the labour
market altogether. Thirdly, the mobility of the family group
was less than the mobility of the individual, whether man,
woman or child.

The history of the nineteenth century in England is the
history of the attempts of capitalism to break down these
social barriers to the cheapening of the raw material of
labour; and, so far as one can see at present, the history of the

twentieth century will be no more than the continuation of these attempts to their complete triumph. Certainly with the exception of ourselves and a mere handful of our readers no group of people anywhere appears in our judgment to be aware of what is actually taking place. On the contrary, as it has been our business, and will continue to be our business to show, the various groups of reformers, all animated presumably by hopes and fears for the nation and the race, are almost without exception aiding and abetting instead of anticipating and hindering the progressive shattering to atoms of our social system. Far from divining the deadly and devilish work in which capitalism is engaged, our Social Reformers in particular, intellectual no less than practical, appear to have divined it only to divinize it; for in every instance that we can recall of a new movement in capitalism for cheapening the raw material of labour still further, the change has been heralded by some social thinker or group of reformers as progressive and liberal, and in many cases has actually been suggested to capitalism by social reformers themselves.

Of these tragical misunderstandings—to use no more sinister term—the break-up of the historic groupings of castes and classes, the parish and local bodies, and the guilds may be cited as comparatively completed examples. There are now, we may say, no castes or classes in England today any more than there are castes or classes in America. Even so recently as fifty years ago Matthew Arnold was able to detect the distinctions—spiritual and not merely material—between what he called the Barbarians, the Philistines and the Populace. But no such distinctions are discernible today. Nothing in the way of principle or quality of mind now divides one class from another. You may find the Barbarian,

the Philistine, and the Populace as readily in Mayfair, at
Oxford, and in Parliament as in the Old Kent Road or
Briggate, Leeds. But with the total disappearance of the distinctions of caste which Arnold saw in their last stages has
emerged the new and definitely capitalist distinction between
the owners of capital and the owners of labour power. These
two classes have, indeed, become defined with terrible
emphasis; and their distinctions are not even yet complete.
Dream it may be, or nightmare rather, but it is with our
waking senses that we appear to behold the increasing segre-
gation of the rich from the poor, the haves from the have-
nots, the owners of land and capital from the raw material
of labour.

But the same reduction to atoms and their rearrangement
under the plutocratic wand have taken place in the sphere of
local groupings, in the sphere of craft groupings, and are
now rapidly taking place in the extreme groupings of the
nation as a whole and the family as a unit. And all, as we
have said, not only without the resistance of the Social Reformers, but largely by their aid. Looking back now on the
wrecks of natural groupings already left by the tide of capitalism, we can see plainly enough that if it was the force of
capitalism that drove these groups upon the rocks, it was the
false lights of the Social Reformers that beckoned them to
their doom. What, for example, but the preaching by the
Social Reformers of the absurdity of class distinctions induced men of the philosophic, artistic, contemplative, political and religious orders to abandon their own principles
and to enter competitive industry—the lowest and vilest
occupation open to mortal man and fit only for the lowest
class in any nation? What, again, was it but the preaching of
the enlightened economist reformers that led to the break-up

of the Guild system, to the establishment of the Manchester system, to Free Trade, to the submerging of the local self-governing groups of parishes and parish districts? In every instance—as we say—the watchword of the army of destruction has been progress. It was progress when the caste system was broken up and its place taken by a plutocratic system. It was progress when the factory system displaced the system of Guilds. It was progress when city manufacture superseded agriculture. It was progress yet once more when government ceased to be local and became centralized in a vast and stupid bureaucracy. But all these things, though led and accompanied by the trumpets of progress, have been only successive steps in the progressive cheapening of the raw material of labour in the interests of capitalism; the proof of which is here and ready to our hand. Never before in the history of England has human labour been as cheap, as abundant, and as excellent in quality as it is today; and never before have Rent, Interest, and Profits been so great. Whatever brains have been responsible for the vast conspiracy of capitalism, at least they are to be applauded for the efficiency of their work. Who would have dreamed who knew the England of the fourteenth, fifteenth and sixteenth centuries that by the end of the nineteenth century only bits of jawbone and fossil teeth would remain of the great institutions which then flourished of the Guild, the local and the caste systems?

But, as we have suggested, the work of capitalism is by no means yet complete. Certain groupings of men have gone, never, perhaps, to be revived, but certain groupings, inimical to capitalism, still remain though under constant attack. Of these the most important are undoubtedly the nation and the family; and both, we fear we must believe, are being shaken in sunder. Consider, for example, what is meant by Internationalism and let us realize how intellectualism of the Liberal variety plays into the hands of Capitalism. Internationalism, we may freely admit, has all the charms of a universal and humane idea. What could be better than to be able to regard each nation of men as distinguished from one's own only by special and cultivated gifts? Or what worse than an insular and curmudgeonly spirit of dislike and distrust of every man not born in our own particular group? That undoubtedly is the appeal of internationalism to the intellectual; but mark how the appeal is utilized by capitalism. The desire of capitalism, likewise, is internationalism, and on a grander scale than anything yet conceived as an aim by any society but the Theosophical Society. The Theosophical Society has for one of its objects the recognition of the brotherhood of men, irrespective of race, creed, colour, caste, or sex. But how does this differ from the object also of the international financier and capitalist? In no respect, save the utilization of the consequent internationalism. For the liberal capitalist one purpose exists and one alone, to reduce the world's supply of the raw material of labour to a condition of complete accessibility, mobility and utility. In his dream of conquest, he sees all human prejudices swept away, all distinctions in men below the possessing classes obliterated, and an open market of the human world, complete free trade in the raw material of labour, established for his profiteering glory. But to this end, as we say, not only does the force of capitalism itself drive, but the light of intellectualism itself beckons. In the name of progress and humanity, we are opening the road for the wreck of nations and for the degradation to the cheapest commodity in the world of the lives of men.

But let us turn now from the largest grouping which men have formed to the smallest; from the nation to the family. At first sight it would appear that here at any rate society had a nucleus which capitalism could not possibly destroy. When we remember that the family system is the oldest natural grouping recorded in the world's history, has survived, by reason of its adaptation to human needs, millions of years' wear and tear, and is associated not only with the health and happiness of the race, but with the religious or ultimate symbol of these—holiness—the assault of capitalism upon the family and the home might seem to be a forlorn hope, an assault at which humanity could well afford to laugh. But let those continue to laugh who are ignorant of what breaches in the historic system of the family have already been made by capitalism and, still worse, what breaches capitalism with the aid of social reformers is now making. We confess that until we came to examine closely the origin of the women's movement, its economic impulses, the facts of the distribution and the present industry of the two adult sections of the proletariat or wage-dependent population, we had only a faint idea of the extent to which the marriage and home and family system has been eaten into by capitalism. We have not the slightest doubt now that the women's movement is economic in its origin, economic in its impulse, and economic (though unbeknown to itself) in its objects. The fact is that capitalism has invaded the home, has broken the ties between men and women, between parents and children, and, in its pursuit of cheap and cheaper labour, has evicted women from the occupation of the home into the streets, there to compete in the world's labour market with men. And the cry of votes for women means no more and no less to us than a cry of Fire. It is a symbol, indeed; a symbol that the capitalist has broken into the home and

turned out its inhabitants and trampled upon their lares and
penates.

We have said that at first sight it would appear as if
neither capitalism nor any other power could have succeeded in breaking down the family; but both the immediate and the recently historical facts are there to convince
us that the miracle is being performed. Not Socialism, as the
imps of the Press pretend, has broken down the family, but
capitalism has already been at the game, as the statistics
prove. It is well known that of the adult population of England the women are in greater proportion than the men.
With the exception of Norway, indeed, England has the
largest population of women relatively to men of any
country in the world. That, as we could easily show, is one
of the effects of capitalism, and of capitalism only. Capitalism has, indeed, as we shall perhaps see in these Notes, a
preference for women—as the weaker sex. In the last resort,
we imagine, capitalism will depend on women's labour. . . .
But not only is there in England an enormous excess of
women over men, but the number of marriages is declining
year by year. Of the twenty million adults, nine and a half
million of whom are women, only seven millions are married. This means that only one in three women has or is
likely to have a home of her own. Now what, we should
like to know, have the aforesaid devilkins of the Press to say
to facts of this kind? Of Socialism as yet we have had in our
legislation not a single trace. The whole of industry is still in
private hands. Yet in spite of this (and because of it, in our
opinion) the family system, together with all that depends
upon it, has been broken down to the extent indicated by
those appalling figures. One in five of our men wage-earners
dies, we are told, a pauper in the workhouse. That is bad

enough. But two out of every three of our women die old maids—whether voluntarily or involuntarily only fools will doubt.

For we are disposed to challenge finally all the idiotic doctrines that have lately been preached both by women and by their men friends in favour of free marriage, free love, no marriage for women at all, no children, no home, no family life, and all the rest of it. All these doctrines are without exception as contrary to the facts of human and divine nature as they are peculiarly pleasing to the demoniac facts of the capitalist system. We shall not be suspected of desiring to praise the so-called anti-Socialist Press when we say that the one useful thing they have done is to combat the spread of these devastating doctrines of certain professing Socialists. Indeed, how can we even give the Press any credit for their attempts in words when at the same time in deeds their capitalist proprietors have been the effective cause of all the destruction of the home of which the Socialists have been merely the apostles and evangels? But that the break-up of the home is anti-natural, however it may be pro-capitalist, there is every warrant both in theory and in fact for affirming. In theory, the settled order of nature is as follows: Man exploits Nature; Woman exploits Man; and Nature exploits Woman. The more this wheel of existence, knit together by mutual services and obligations, is examined the more it will appear that we have here not one of what the "Nation" calls the "juvenile paradoxes" of *The New Age*, but one of the oldest and most settled facts of the world. This particular order, indeed, may be said to be the wheel of life itself. Interrupt it at any point, attempt to reverse it, or introduce another form of activity into it, the effect may be wonderful, it may even be (we do not deny) mystically transcendent, but life as we know it, and human life as it is, will certainly cease, to the extent of our interference, to exist. But it is precisely an interference, and that in its worst form, that capitalism introduces into this Wheel of Life. In the first place, no capitalist really exploits Nature at all; he exploits men. Not his to wrest from Nature by his brain and hand the wealth she hoards; but like the great Whore of Babylon (his mythical prototype), it is his to wrest from men who themselves exploit Nature, the cream of their conquest. Not his, again, to maintain the order of things that allows both men and women the innocent and mutually beneficent exploitation of the man by the woman. On the contrary, it is just his skua-bird work to snatch from women their natural right of exploiting men and to employ it in competition with them on his own behalf. Maintaining the order of Nature, indeed! Why, capitalism reverses the order at every point, lives by parasitism on Nature, on Men and on Women alike, robs everybody in the world and everything; and for what service to a living soul in return? Let our slums lift up their voice; let our nation utter its word; let the dumb artists, thinkers, poets and philosophers make their gestures of despair. For no service save to themselves have capitalists done all these things.

So much of the theory, but the actual facts testify to no less a wrong to men and women than to the order of Nature. We were recently asked by a correspondent to affirm, if we dared, that women are naturally economically dependent upon men and desire so to remain. Well, we dare to affirm it, for it is true in spite of all the loud propaganda of the contrary. The shrill pipers of the "Freewoman" and the eunuchs of both sexes who advocate the economic independence of woman have, we charitably suppose, no notion of the unhappiness that they are endeavouring to allay by still more unhappy means. Nevertheless it is a fact which we invite the experienced to confirm that not only is the average woman constituted by nature and genuine disposition to live econo-mically dependent upon man, but both she and a man are happier in that relation, more self-respecting and more honourable in each other's eyes. We have never met a man yet who did not secretly pride himself on the number of women he could support—be they his relatives or his mis-tresses. On the other hand, we have never met the woman yet (and we hope we never shall) who did not regard the exchange of economic dependence upon an employer for economic dependence upon a man as an honourable pro-motion. What is the use of women or of men either lying to themselves and each other about these facts? It is not we who have invented them; it is not lying that can alter them. The true truth is, and the facts are there to prove it, that a society in which marriage is declining is a society in which health and happiness are declining; that a society which either makes it impossible for a man to keep a woman (two if he likes), or makes it necessary for a woman to keep herself, is a declining society; and, finally, that women when they are driven from the exploitation of men to the exploitation of Nature on behalf of capitalists are degrading themselves in Nature's eyes, in men's eyes and in their own eyes, even though they call the degradation freedom and emancipation.

But in order to see that the present position of women is due to capitalism and nothing else, and that from this point of view the women's movement in its professed objects is a capitalist movement for the further cheapening of the raw material of labour, let us follow out the steps by which women have been driven to impale men upon this dilemma.

The pursuit of capitalists being, as we say, the cheapening of labour among the rest of its raw materials, it follows that in the normal course of its development the wages of men will tend to fall to the subsistence level of their lowest efficient and sufficient class. At every step in the competition of capitalism for profits and of wage-labourers for a living, each party will be compelled to break down, the one every obstacle to cheapness, and the other every obstacle to his continuing to live. The capitalist, on the one hand, will open up labour supplies in every class or nation or race possible to him, with the sole idea of buying his raw material on free-trade terms in the cheapest market. At the same time he will exert his influence to destroy any taboos, natural or artificial, on the entrance of any class into his industrial system. Again, he will endeavour to extract by economy in use the utmost value to himself of every single wage-earning individual. Finally, he will seek even cheaper substitutes for human labour in the form of machinery and natural forces. But with the enlargement of the supply of labour consequent on his exertions, the wage-labourers, on the other hand, find their value in the labour market of supply and demand diminishing. To maintain themselves at all they must be prepared, slowly but surely, to come down in their demands to the level of the least exigent of their competitors. But under internationalism, the competitors of English workmen are not merely English workmen, but the workers of the world. What the Chinese, let us say, can live upon, that, in no long time, if international capitalism concludes its labours before international Socialism has begun its mission, the English working man must live upon also. It is obvious that garment by garment, luxury by luxury, indulgence by indulgence, tradition by tradition, the English wage-earner must strip himself of every superfluous expense in order to contract the sum of his demands within the competitive minimum on which his value in industry is based. And not only of superfluities must he be prepared to strip himself, but afterwards of necessities in the order of their indispensability. At present, we may suppose, he fancies himself as requiring a wife and children and a house in which to lodge them. But that is only a fancy for capitalism, which prefers a man without encumbrances. The man resists? His place is taken by another without that fancy. Result: A marrying man is displaced; and a marriageable woman is thrown on to the streets or into the mill.

At the same time that this cheapening of men's labour is going on, making it increasingly difficult for a man to keep his mother or his sisters or a wife and family, these latter, as we have seen, are being pushed into the labour market there to compete with the only person whose wages it is their business to maintain. For by a natural concatenation of effects, as fast almost as these women come into the labour market, industry becomes more and more adapted to them and less and less to men. We have seen that, as a matter of fact, the number of women is increasing in England faster than that of men. What is more natural under the circumstances? With the development of automatic machinery, with the division of labour, with the decay of agriculture, the crafts and manly occupations of all kinds—above all, with the substitution in industry of women for men, the demand for men in industry declines at the same time that the demand for women in industry rises. We agree that at present women are unskilled in industry as well as naturally indisposed to it, but we do not agree that they must always remain so. On the contrary, having seen what capitalism can do in the sphere of the nation, the guild, the home, we enter-tain no doubt that it can bend, if not change radically, the human nature of women to its will. Women, there is no doubt about it, will fall as readily into wage-slavery as men have fallen before them; and to the extent that they fall not only will men go with them, but men will actually precede them in their lowest descent. Nor are we, in all this, speculating merely in the dark folds of the prophet's mantle. The facts are open before the world; the deductions we have made can be checked and verified or contradicted and ignored if they are wrong. Let nobody suppose that we are attempting by journalistic means to make the flesh of our readers creep. What have we to gain by shaking and shocking the allegiance of the last surviving band of honest inquirers after truth? If we are wrong in our deductions, so much the happier shall we be.

In this war of capitalism on what we have called the settled facts of human nature, sinister casualties beyond the pen of the present writer to describe occur in thousands. We can only refer briefly to a few of them. Our contributor "M. B. Oxon" has lately been making an appeal for a more liberal understanding of the obligations of sex. But it is plain that capitalism which prevents marriage and decent prostitution drives the sexual appetite to indulge itself merely on the cheap. It is well known that cheap prostitution and even cheaper fornication are the invariable accompaniments of the cheap wage-labour of men and women. Who are the damned bishops to hold their noses when this is said? Or the Vigilance Committees consisting mostly of wealthy brutes, each with his harem of mistresses? Or the squalidly pure-minded editors who support capitalism with one hand and endeavour to suppress its droppings with the other? The decline of men's wages under the competitive system is as certain to be followed by the decline of marriage and the rise of free fornication and cheap prostitution for the masses of women as day is to be followed by night. Men and women, lord bishops and vigilance committees and editors, were animals first, and will be animals again when their human status is taken away. Humanity, we repeat, is maintained by an effort, by an effort of society. Relax that effort, as our capitalists have done, rob civilization of its store of common human treasure, and man rattles into barbarism as fast as his two legs can become four. Immorality and the degradation of the race, we say for the tenth time, are the inevitable consequences of capitalism. Not all the preaching, teaching and idealism in the world will alter that simple fact.

But as sinister and barbarous in our view are the correlative effects of capitalism on our intellectuals. The plain features of the existing situation stare these brainy persons, these brilliant mountebanks, in the face if only their eyes were in their heads. Capitalism, we say, is driving men out of industry, and as it drives them out it is inviting in the still cheaper labour of women. What is there in women that so commends them to the great Whore of Capitalist Babylon? Listen. They are cheaper because their standard of living is less. They have no man to maintain—no man would be maintained by them. Their industrial vices are few and small. They are more docile to managerial discipline. They are newer to the game. They are less disposed to combination among themselves than men. They are incapable of collective violence, and their individual violence is negligible. They are better machines. Are not these qualities sufficient to procure them a ready admission into industry? But men, you say, will never submit to this importation into their industry of so much cheap labour; the women, too, will see that their entrance will be over the corpses of marriage, morality, and the family life. But we are reckoning without our intellectuals, our Ibsens, and Shaws, and Wells. At the very moment that capitalism is invading the home and battering it down from without to extract therefrom the cheapest labour England provides (women and children), our intellectuals engage themselves either in battering it down from within or in mingling their ineffectual tears and promises with the cries of despair of its inmates. The economic independence of women! The emancipation of women from the thraldom of marriage! Free feeding for children! The endowment of maternity! Sexual promiscuity free gratis and for everybody! Down with the sanctity of marriage, the home and the family! . . . We understand now very well why intellectuals like Mr. Shaw and Mr. Wells make money by their writings and their plays. All unwittingly, no doubt, and in pursuit of a living, these poor creatures are assisting the dehumanizing work of capitalists. As doctrines for the esoteric, for intellectuals, in fact, we have no objection to the theories of Mr. Shaw and Mr. Wells. They may be preached by practice and by practice only; but as contributions to society, the effect of their work is unmistakably to pave the way for the admission of women into wage-slavery and for the ejection of men from existence altogether. We do not expect either Mr. Shaw or Mr. Wells to reply to our charges. There is no reply. We are content to leave the matter to their intellectual consciences with this one hope: that they may both live long enough to see themselves derided and their accursed doctrines numbered among the fads of the early twentieth century.

We have shown now, we hope, as clearly as our space will allow, the origin of the women's movement in capital-

D

ism, and the futility as well as brilliant stupidity of the remedies suggested for it, namely, the entrance of women into wage-slavery and the substitution of capitalist stud-farms and free fornication (however disguised) for the natural institution of the home. But let us see now how the women themselves and the men's Labour Party face the situation and what may be expected if their suggestions are carried out. Among the women posing in the movement as representatives of their sex (though they are no more representative of their sex than Mr. Shaw is of his), two distinct lines of "advance" are advocated. One, as we all know, is the capture of the political vote; the other, and a more sensible one, is the capture by women of the industrial market. Now we say that of these two professed objects of women both are bad, but one is worse than the other. It is bad in our opinion for the reasons we have given that women should enter the industrial market *while wage-slavery prevails there.* The only possible effect of their incursion will be to reduce wages to their level of subsistence and to depreciate marriage and morality in necessary consequence. On the other hand, if women are actually about to act upon a lie—the lie, namely, that they prefer an employer to a man—the more thoroughly they do it the sooner will the tragedy of our race reach its climax. By all means, therefore, if wage-earners will not end wage-slavery and make enough to enable them to keep women, let women enter industry themselves even if it involves turning men out. That, we say, is sensible folly, if folly can have any sense. It is at least practical. But the other line of "advance", the capture of the vote, is folly, senseless folly and impracticable folly. It does not say much for the intelligence of women that at a time when they should be anxiously employed in speculating how they may get a living, they should be treading down each other for the capture of a vote. With the marriage market declining and the wage-level of all industry going down, the chances of getting a man to keep them or an employer to pay them a decent living wage are obviously declining too. Is it the time to attempt to obtain a political feather for their hat when at any moment they may find themselves without a hat to put it in? For we have proved as patiently, persistently, and clearly as we can, that political action is never at any time a cause of economic action, but an effect of it. Imagine thirteen million Sindbads ridden by a million Old Men of the Sea, each securely ensconced upon his respective wage-earners' shoulders; and imagine, then, those thirteen million passing resolutions to determine what their million Riders of the Sea shall do—that is a true picture of the relation of politics to economics. It is scarcely to be expected that if seven million men with all their votes have failed to overturn the capitalist system, the addition of seven million women will bring about the revolution. On the contrary . . . as capitalists very well know! Are they not nicely divided in their views upon Women's Suffrage? Lord Cowdray may oppose Mr. Kenny of the *Daily Herald*; but both Lady Cowdray and Lord Cowdray may support Mr. Kenny's sister of "Votes for Women" fame. Why? Are the capitalists so anxious that women should get a living at the same time that men are ceasing to be able to live and they care nothing? Nonsense. The capitalists are divided on Women's Suffrage, because Women's Suffrage is an indifferent thing. On the cheapening of labour, however, they are united in an indivisible brotherhood that does Nonconformists and devils good to see.

If there is no hope in the remedial means put forward by the women . . . hope in the remedial means put forward by Mr. Shaw and Mr. Wells, whither shall we turn as sincere

feminists for real help for women? It might be thought that
suffering from the same system of capitalism as men, even
though in an indirect way, suffering also under men's eyes
as their mothers, sisters, wives and daughters, the women
might expect real and manly advice and assistance from the
Labour Party. But we know our Labour leaders and our
Labour Party. To a man they are women every one. The
she-Labour Party we called them once, and well they have
earned the name. For we have to note that having completely failed in economics to provide as fathers, husbands,
sons and brothers for their women folk they are now on the
knees of the House of Commons to beg for pensions, insurance against sickness and all the other perquisites of faded
mistresses. We wonder that the men they represent in this
ignominious attitude do not burst with wrath to see their
fellows holding the begging-bowl in Parliament as a diversion from holding the collection plate in the tabernacle.
Begging, begging, it is all begging! And it is from a party of
beggars like this that the women are to derive their champions. Let us say at once that under no conceivable circumstances can the Labour Party by political means advance the
women's cause either actually or even fallaciously. Observers
make a great mistake who suppose that a party holding even
the balance of power in Parliament are necessarily powerful.
They are powerful in those matters only on which a division
of opinion between the two capitalist parties harmlessly
exists; and these, without exception, are small matters, however large they are made to loom in the steam from the
witch's cauldron of the Press. But on vital matters in politics
the Labour Party has exactly and no more than the pull of its
economic strength. As necessary as English labour is to
English capital so influential is the Labour Party in the
capitalist Parliament. Nobody can deny it.

But actually, as we have seen, the Labour Party can neither in theory nor in practice assist the women to economic independence either without at the same time undermining still further the economic independence of their men wage-earning constituents. This, if we have proved nothing else, is at least as clear as daylight. We have seen that the reduction of wages brought about by capitalism in its pursuit of cheaper raw material has resulted in making it impossible for a *majority* of the lower wage-earners to marry or to keep any women folk whatever. We have seen, further, that in consequence of this impoverishment by capitalism of the breadwinner, the women are turning out into the streets to demand, by name, votes and employers, but silently men. Now what can the Labour Party do for women under these circumstances? They cannot give them the vote, though they may promise them it; and even if they gave them the vote, the women would be no nearer getting a living. On the other hand, if they assist women into wage-slavery, not only will women have nothing to thank them for, but the men themselves will find their own wages still further reduced. This, again, is not mere prophecy: the facts are growing under our eyes. For good or for ill, for better or for worse, the men will discover that in aiding and abetting the women's movement by attempting to satisfy either of its professed objects, they are actually cutting their own throats and the women's throats as well. Suppose, we say, that nine or ten millions of Chinese were to present through their ambassador a demand to be admitted to the English labour market to compete with men—what would the English Labour Party, in spite of its internationalism, its Christian brotherhood and its pacifism, do then? We cannot see even its most brainless members welcoming the importation and going out to salute with banners the pigtailed horde. Yet, so far as industry is concerned, the invasion of women, with their cry of "All labour for our province", differs in no respect whatever from an invasion of cheap Chinese. The competition of women in the labour market to-day (and more and more as machinery expands) is as certain as a Chinese coolie invasion to reduce men's wages and to bring wages in general down to the weakest and most self-sacrificing woman's bare necessities. Is that, we ask, what the Labour Party really intend by their infatuate advocacy of the women's cause *in the women's way*? Intended or not, as surely as women are allowed to enter wage-industry on a large scale, so surely will men's wages fall. The laws of the Medes and Persians are not more certain.

Again we dwell, perhaps unduly, on this phase of our argument, for the point is one of the utmost importance. What is the fundamental difference between the women's movement and the Labour movement? Both, we admit, are economic in their origin. Both, we maintain, are products of capitalism, and both are susceptible of a single remedy, an economic remedy. But though the root causes of the two movements are identical, one is, as it were, subsidiary to and consequent upon the other. The men's movement, that is, owes its origin directly to capitalism, but the women's movement owes its origin to capitalism only indirectly and through men. If there had been no necessity for a men's labour movement it is certain that there would have been no necessity for a woman's political and economic movement. A woman's spiritual or intellectual movement very likely— they need one badly enough—but an economic movement, never! But this suggests what is the real difference between the objects of the movements as distinct from their common cause. The real object of the women's movement in so far as its economic intentions are realized, is to enter the industrial system, to take service under private capitalists and to get into the wage system. But the real object of the Labour movement is precisely the opposite: it is to get away from the industrial system, to throw off private capitalists and to abolish the wage-system. Our readers will see at once that the objects of the two movements are, in fact, not only incompatible, but they are contrary in direction. Here are the men in wage-slavery trying in vain to get out; and here are the women trying in vain to get in! It is an occupation for minor poets, those lovers of dirty tragedies, to watch the men struggling out chivalrously assisting the women to struggle in. Oh, you stocks, you stones, you anything but men! Can you not see when it is pointed out to you, that you are inviting the women to their ruin and to your own as well? . . . A few of Mr. Wells's unspeakable dots, for the love of God.

But if it is true, as it *is* true, that the women's movement is a consequence and not merely a coincidence of the Labour movement, it surely follows that the real remedy for the women's grievance is consequent upon and is included in the remedy for the men's grievance. To this conclusion, indeed, all our reasonings, we trust, have been steadily pointing. As a diagnosis of the situation in which women unhappily find themselves we boldly announce that their disease is men's low wages. That and that alone is the root of all their present trouble. But does it not follow again from this that the remedy for their trouble is the remedy of higher wages for men? We think it does, and we challenge any of our bitterest critics to state publicly in what link our chain of reasoning is weak, if it should appear to them to have ended in a "juvenile paradox". For what else but the ending of capitalism and the abolition of the competitive wage system can conceivably free women from the peril of their present hellish choice between a husband with insufficient wages for himself and the family and an employer who will pay her less than she can comfortably live upon and rob her of a man into the bargain? Is it in the preaching of the sanctity of marriage? There will soon be no marriages among the poor to be made holy. Marriage will shortly become one of the moral and inaccessible luxuries of the capitalist classes distinguishing them in the sight of the Church from the immoral beasts who fornicate in our slums.

Is it in the Endowment of Motherhood or in State provision and parentage for children? To substitute a bureaucrat for a father in one aspect will infallibly be to substitute a bureaucracy for natural parentage in general. In other words we shall be plump into State Eugenics with Dr. Saleeby and Mr. Montagu Crackanthorpe as the selectors of the human mares and stallions. But Mr. G. K. Chesterton puts his faith in democracy! And Dr. Oscar Levy puts his faith in aristocracy! They are wrong, both of them, though we say it with our compliments. Democracy, we must impress upon Mr. Chesterton, has so far failed to maintain a single one of its outposts against the attack of Capitalism with its big battalions. The natural democratic groupings, which we thought so stable, of the parish, the district, the guild and even the "pub", have gone down one by one, and the Church their Mother with them, in the first encounter with the international capitalist. And already we have begun to see the most ancient of our institutions, the nation and the family, losing their integrity, suffering in their morale and dwindling in cohesion as well as in numbers without evoking a real protest from the massed millions of our people. On the con-

trary, where our capitalists lead there our intellectuals follow; and where our intellectuals lead the people also follow.
Democracy, we fear, is the first resort, and it has proved
useless. Our people will suffer extinction rather than fight for
the rights a sturdier generation won for them. But an aristocracy, what of that? A first-rate, splendid, philosophic
aristocracy founded upon docile, efficient, universal wage-
slavery! But Dr. Levy is not so wanting in profundity that he
fails to see that an aristocracy cannot be founded or imposed
or drawn out from a plutocracy. Silk purses are not made of
sows' ears. The very qualities which constitute and maintain
a plutocracy are qualities inimical even to the existence of an
aristocracy. We know that at this moment it is as much as
any natural aristocrat (and they are scattered like lost sheep
over all our classes) can do to breathe in the fetid atmosphere
of wealth production and of wealth squandering. Let the
division of wealth and labour continue inequitable as now;
let the inequity increase but a little; down the gulf between
the two classes will sink every virtue, every noble quality,
every art, every human beauty that has ever flourished in
our common civilization. Mob at the top and mob below.
Dr. Levy's Nietzsche has already said it. But the description
will prove to be flattering to the top and the below of society
when wealth has further accumulated and men have further
decayed. Returning to the subject of the women's movement
we say that there is no remedy for women's grievance apart
from men's. Whatever increases men's wages will at the
same time allay the fever of women. Double men's wages
to-morrow, and the women's movement would die in
euthanasia the day after. This is true, our readers will learn,
though everybody should rise to contradict it. It is the true
truth about the women's movement.

August 29, 1912.

THE NEW ENGLISH WEEKLY

INTRODUCTION

The World Today

If our civilization must perish it will not be because
of ignorance of what is needed to save it; and, in that sense,
it may be claimed that the cause of Civilization is not yet
entirely lost. On the other hand, the fact that the patient
appears to be dying within easy reach of cure is itself perhaps
the most alarming symptom of disease of all. Civilizations
before us have died in the midst of their ignorance; but our
own Civilization, if it is doomed to perish, will have the evil
distinction in history of dying not only with the cure at hand
but on the eve of such a life as has never been known since
the days of Eden; on the eve, in short, of the possible realization of the promise of the Golden Age. And it is this attitude
of resistance to cure, of willessness in the presence of a potentially glorious future, that may prove to be one of the fatal
symptoms of our present epoch. The successful conspiracy
of the mediocre against the able which is the typical symptom of decadence, and of this age in England, may easily
ruin us even in a period of profound peace. A war would
merely prove it. IV 13

Civilization, though apparently stricken unto death, may,
on the other hand, be actually pregnant of a new epoch; and,
with our limited experience of the development of Man, we
may easily be mistaking the symptoms of renaissance for the
signs of approaching dissolution. We have not the smallest
doubt ourselves that the problem now facing Civilization is

61

critical and a matter of life and death; nor can there be in any intelligent mind the smallest doubt of the nature of that problem. It is the problem of combining Personal Liberty with the distribution of Plenty. Now the solution of that problem is known, it is accessible and it is immediately applicable. Whether, however, the dark forces incarnated in human greed of power, pride of place and contempt for humanity, may not contrive to hide the saving formula and by precipitating another war procure an abortion—that neither we nor anybody can know. But the mere washing of hands will exempt nobody from responsibility.　　II 14

We feel, in the presence of the orthodox economists and politicians of today, rather like Columbus in the presence of Isabella. Is it possible, we ask ourselves, that the news has not reached them or, having reached them, has not been realized, that the New World of Plenty actually exists, and that the psychology of Scarcity, together with the Economics and Sociology based upon it, is now only at best a superstitious survival and at worst of the order of devil-worship? The facts, if facts are allowed to speak, can speak eloquently for themselves. Thanks to Science and Invention and Engineers, there is now not a single article of human use that can be made or grown the potential supply of which is not practically unlimited, and, moreover, at a cost in human labour that would leave ample leisure for culture to every member of the human family. This is not merely a new fact in the history of the world, and an actual fact at this moment, but it will continue and become more patent with time unless some cataclysm of Nature or man's folly occurs to put an end to it. Thanks to the potency of the same seed from which the Industrial Beanstalk has already sprung, its growth will continue indefinitely and, we might almost say, remorselessly. The Age of Plenty is upon us, and mankind must either adapt its polity to it or suffer even worse ills than those of the past and passing Age of Scarcity.

This picture of fact, however, must be set side by side with another picture which we will leave Lord Revelstoke to draw. Speaking in the City, very impressively according to the dramatic critics who write the financial columns of the Press, Lord Revelstoke described the world as "writhing in a purgatory of its own making". "We see", he continued, "the stream of international commerce which is said to require, for its normal flow, some 400 millions of fresh credit every year, reduced to a trickle . . . the price of goods having fallen below the cost of production. We see these goods losing value daily, because they have ceased, or nearly ceased, to change hands. We see the burden of debts and of taxation intensified to breaking point, solvent debtors in default, banking facilities at a standstill. We see the delicate mechanism of exchange crippled by arbitrary control, barter between Governments supplanting the effort of individual traders, foodstuffs being destroyed in despair, warehouses glutted with a surplus which is only redundant because the consuming power of millions of people has been either frustrated or paralysed. Worse than all, we see standards of honour debased, and goodwill, the leaven which ought to permeate humanity, slowly perishing; while distrust, that fear of our neighbour which it is the mission of Christianity to dispel, spreads like a pestilence from day to day." Lord Revelstoke's picture, like that in the preceding paragraph, is not in the least degree overdrawn. The two hang side by side like photographs in contrast, each indubitably realistic— the one, however, to the glory, and the other to the shame of Man. For there need not be the smallest doubt that the paradox of Plenty, of which these two pictures are the illustration, is no longer even a problem to men of intelligence. As certainly as scientists can affirm today that the problem of, let us say, mechanical flight that seemed insoluble no longer ago than a quarter of a century is conclusively and practically solved, any competent economist today can affirm and prove that the problem of adjusting Demand to Supply, Consumption to Production, Scarcity to Plenty, has ceased to be a problem in theory and need not be a problem in practice for longer than a few months at the very outside.

The difficulties in the way of practice, however, are unfortunately anything but negligible or easily superable. Such prejudices have grown up both from humanity's long experience of Scarcity and from the semi-magical associations of Money, that between the two of them only the strongest minds can be depended upon to be able to think straight. It is almost as if the barest suggestion of a relation between Plenty and Money were enough to disorder men's minds so that they ceased to be able to function intelligently. To the competent observer, fully aware that all that is wrong with the existing order—Capitalism, if you will—is a relatively minor failure to expand and distribute purchasing power step by step with productive capacity—a failure due simply to the fact that Adam Smith wrote our economic Old Testament before Watts inaugurated the age of steam and electricity—the spectacle of a world writhing in the agony of the strait-waistcoat of Money shortage while doomed to continue to expand productively is a paradox of comedy and tragedy. In comparison with this world-spectacle there is nothing that can even be said to be of much importance, since every detail of our social picture is scaled and coloured in relation to the whole. Art, religion and culture, education and sociology generally, world-peace, internationalism, the whole future of mankind on this planet, all alike depend on our ability to face up to and practically solve the problem presented to the race for the first time in its history—the problem, simply stated and, as we have said, in theoretic solution equally simple, of creating and distributing purchasing-power *pari passu* with our expanding means of production. The fundamental problem, we repeat, is one of Money, since Science has settled every other; and there is no problem of the world today whose solution does not depend upon it.

Once seen as the central question for civilization that it is, the problem of adapting our Money-system to our Productive-system ought to brook and can brook of no dispensable delay, still less of wilful or merely ignorant obscurantism. Unfortunately, there is no Chairman to preside over world-debates and to call to order partisan speakers and to rule out irrelevant contributions. Every man must do it for himself. But it should be possible at least in a limited forum to pre-serve the conventions of great debate and, above all, upon a matter of practical policy upon the decision of which human fate depends.

The outstanding feature of world economics today is the growing tendency towards the self-sufficiency of nations of which, as usual, merely political nationalism is only the articulate symptom. Assuredly it is too early to declare that "economic nationalism" is already a practical possibility—at any rate, for more than one or two nations; but it is not too early to declare, with prophetic certainty, that the Free Trade dream of economic internationalism is no longer even theoretically realizable, and that, if not today then to-morrow, every adult nation will aim at being at least so far independent as to be able to function as an integral unit in the world, as a partner in it and not as a mere part of it. Nor is this aim, as Free Traders contend, an objective to be de-

E

plored, any more than it is the result of "tariff" propaganda. It stands to reason that as Industrialism spreads in ever-widening and intensifying waves, every national unit will, as far as it is able, and as soon as it can, instrument itself for its own support. An international trade that was predominantly important while nations were, so to say, stocking themselves with the means of production, must begin to decline in relative importance just as soon as each nation begins to be able to manufacture for itself. And unless, therefore, at a time such as has now come, when nations, feeling their feet, begin to depend less and less upon foreign trade and more and more upon the home-market—unless, we say, at such a time, nations can learn how to develop their home-market to absorb what before was exported, they must either resume an era of foreign wars to force their goods down unwilling foreign throats or choke at home on their own undistributed goods. We are announcing nothing new when we announce the approaching end of International Trade as a major factor in modern life.   I 1

Our gargantuan Productive resources are the result of the gift of God and the genius of Man; but their present distribution for the purposes of Consumption can only be regarded as the curse of the Devil aided and abetted by the stupidity and folly of Man. To overcome the latter, and, while leaving Production to go its own splendidly fruitful way, to devise a means of enabling the community, and ultimately the whole world, to enter in and possess and enjoy the Promised Land of Plenty—that, we say, is still the hope before us.

III 21

The Economic Design of Society

Without a working knowledge of the financial and economic design in the conduct of foreign policy, the ordinary observer is in the position of seeing only the wrong side of the tapestry; and, naturally enough, the odd ends and knots that come under his observation either fail to make a picture at all and leave him bewildered, or, worse still, suggest a picture that is grotesquely misleading. On the other hand, the design itself, even when shown to them, is for the majority of people too simple to be believed: as Heraclitus said of the truth, it escapes belief by its credibility. Who can believe, for example, that the only design in modern domestic government is the maintenance and extension of the power of the Money Monopoly? And, correspondingly, that the only design in the foreign policy which proceeds from it, is the financial hegemony of the world? To our manufacturers, no doubt, it is made to appear that the question at issue is world-trade in their own concrete sense of the word: England's continued supremacy in the world-market of goods, on the naive assumption that England lives by her exports. But it should be obvious on even a little reflection that a policy that has consistently encouraged foreign competitors by financing them with the most up-to-date machinery and technique, and still continues to do so, is not primarily concerned with England's supremacy in point of the world-market in goods, but rather with Money's supremacy everywhere and anywhere. And the same considerations may be said to apply in the political field also. What, for instance, is the explanation, from the political point of view, of the volte face of the Government in its attitude to Russia? It is clear, in the first place, that the published terms of our recent Trade Agreement with Russia are of such a nature that no one can be deceived by them; with all the propaganda in the world they cannot be made to appear as more than an affair between grocers. It is no less clear that the political implications of the Agreement are of the same order of camouflage; since it was no less obvious ten years ago than it was last week that (as *The Times* says) "it is impossible to keep a great country like Russia in an isolation ward", and that "the worst features of Bolshevism are more likely to be mitigated by facilitating intercourse between Russia and the outside world than by attempts at boycott". Why, then, we ask, have these truths become obvious just at this moment? What is the design that now dictates their admission after their long denial? Once again we point to considerations beyond mere politics and even beyond economics as ordinarily understood: to a financial policy directed, for the moment, against Japan. For in the event that Japan should decline to enter the ring, or demand too high a price for inclusion, it is only elementary policy to be prepared with an alternative; and the alternative demands friendship with Russia—Vladivostock being only four hundred miles from Tokyo.   IV 20

During the last thirty years or more—and particularly since the Great War gave impetus to every description of self-seeking and "graft"—quite a new conception of political and public life seems to have taken hold of this nation. The rush and scramble of life—the fight for a living which is the common lot of an increasing majority of our people— the daily babel of sensationalism served up by a modern Press controlled by "interests" and only concerned with circulation and profit-earning—these and similar influences have been steadily undermining national character, making us insensible to the dangers before our eyes. Commercial corruption—evidenced by one financial scandal following another in rapid succession—has come to be recognized as an inevitable concomitant of our commercial system: the "Parliamentary" answer—the lie told in Parliament to avoid disclosure of the truth—has been accepted as an everyday feature of our representative system, and so the drift continues. How long the nation will tolerate it we dare not guess. For our own part we think the nation really desires to know the truth of what is going on behind the scenes. Our national indignation moves slowly in such matters. We are apt to believe what we want to believe, and we do not like to believe that evil exists in any direction until we are forced to admit and believe it.   V 13

The Money Factor

The following simplified statements are incontrovertible. 1. Money is the most important commodity in modern society, since it legally commands all others. 2. The quantity of Money in circulation determines the price-level of all other commodities. 3. The manufacture of the commodity Money is a Monopoly of the Central Bank of any given credit-area, e.g. of the Bank of England for England. 4. The quantity of Money in circulation at any given moment is determined by the Central Bank. 5. This quantity, as to its maximum, is arbitrarily fixed at a multiple, in this country, of the Fiduciary Issue plus the Gold holding of the Bank of England, and, as to its minimum, by the Fiduciary issue alone. 6. The variations of quantity between these two limits, brought about by Inflation or Deflation, or the issue and cancellation of credit, have no necessary relation with the facts of Industry as a whole, but only with the exigencies of the money-market. 7. Since such variations vitally affect Industry by affecting the price-level of all commodities Industry is compelled to reflect the facts of the Bank of

England's money-policy and to expand or contract as the Bank expands or contracts the quantity of Money in circulation. 8. This subordination of all Industry to the Money industry is at the root of the world's economic misery. 9. The proper function of a Money-system is to reflect the facts of Industry, and not vice versa; that is to say the quantity of Money circulating within any given credit-area should expand only with Production and contract only with Consumption. 10. In these conditions any given community or credit-area would always have complete monetary control over its industrial resources. 11. The Treasury is the national authority for putting such a system into operation. 12. The resistance to the adoption of such a monetary system is ultimately that of the present privileged Monopolists of Money.   I 10

The fundamental fact of Economics is that the National Wealth begins with and for ever depends upon the actual worth of the individual citizens. There is no wealth but life. In the financial exploitation of Watts's discovery of the use of Steam, the world has failed to remember that, in the end, the most marvellous machine of the most marvellous forces is Man himself; and that the subordination of Man to the machines of his own invention is a diabolical inversion not only of all humane values, but of strictly economic values as well. It is an anguish to the few normal human beings amongst us to witness the steady deterioration of men side by side with the steady development of machinery. The sacrifice of cultural values is on a scale to call for the wrath of God. But, even on the plane of economic values—the capacity to produce and deliver Goods where, when and as wanted—the multiplication of A1 machines at the cost of the multiplication of C3 men cannot be regarded as itself more than the economics of a madhouse.   IV 26

It is possible, indeed, as our easily satisfied statesmen are always claiming, that the state of England may, in comparison with that of other nations, appear to be, even if it is actually not, tolerable. Communities as different from England as Iceland and Switzerland, where Communist riots have been taking place before even the leaves are sere, are not only suffering with England, America and Germany, but exhibiting the same symptoms and receiving at the hands of their financial advisers the same poisonous prescriptions. Nobody worth the appellation human can believe that local, temporary or temperamental causes are to blame for a phenomenon so universal. Nobody, again, with any mind at all, can fail to see and realize the paradox in which the world is at losing grips. Plenty, plenty, bursting plenty of everything save monetary tickets of admission to the feast exists; and only the beastly ignorance of the Money Monopolists and their crew stands between the world and its material happiness.   II 5

The Chronic Nature of Economic Crisis

We have to confess, with an increasing body of observers, that even in our most *laisser faire* moments, we cannot discern a single sign that the situation will clear up of itself or even that it will remain no worse than it is. The forces now in operation are, we believe, exceptional. There have never been anything like them in the total experience of mankind. And the crisis to which they have brought us is not a passing phenomenon but the point of culmination and concentration of processes which, unless given a complete change of direction, will infallibly destroy civilization.

In no circumstances, present or prospective, visible to reason, is it conceivable that, with the world's monetary gold distributed as it is and where it is, this country of England can ever again return to the Gold Standard, unless our City and Treasury are prepared to reduce England to the status of an American colony under the mandate of the Federal Reserve Bank. Surely it is not necessary to argue the case. The facts speak for themselves. And the inevitable conclusion is that the sooner this country announces its decision never to return to the Gold Standard the sooner will the world-situation begin to be cleared up.

Everybody is, of course, now fully aware that the suspension of international lending, chiefly by America, was mainly responsible for the precipitation of the present prolonged crisis. The world's debtors were unable to continue paying their creditors when the latter ceased supplying them with the means. But to imagine that the reversal of the process by the resumption of international long-term lending is either possible or, if made, would affect any radical improvement in the situation, is also to imagine that the suspension of international lending, on the part of America, was an arbitrary and, so to say, voluntary act. In the realm of theory, no doubt, where most "practical" financiers and economists live, it is perhaps natural to suppose that all that is necessary to restore international lending and the one-way trade it involves (the so-called favourable balance) is confidence coupled with, in the case of America, a little more "experience" in handling world finance. But apart from the absurdity of reproaching American financiers with "inexperience", in view of their present advantage, it is absurd to assume that their decision to cease lending abroad was a mere whim. The decision to cease lending abroad was, in fact, not a decision at all, but a result of circumstances inherent in the situation itself. And it is exactly comparable to the behaviour of our domestic banks in "ceasing" to extend credits at home. The fact is that would-be borrowers, nations or individuals, ceased to be able to offer any security and became thereby automatically "uncreditworthy", with the natural and inevitable consequence that lending ceased.

Not only are the nation's worries not over, even if they are packed up in its kit-bag, but they are only, as it were, beginning. We are in the early months only, and possibly weeks, of the Greatest war of all time—the war between an inexorable Machine and the human spirit. And, moreover, if our national victory is to depend upon lending our customers money with which to buy from us, and then arranging the Money-system to enable them to sell their Goods to us at the highest possible price, the victory itself will cost us both our money and our lives.   II.11

The Cause of Crisis

The fundamental cause of the breakdown in America and, eventually, in all the rest of the world, is to be looked for and found in the systematic creation of an increasing disparity between the physical means of Production and the financial means of Consumption. The actual purchasing-power distributed in the form of Wages is increasingly insufficient to buy the Production at Cost-price, with the consequence that this deficiency of purchasing-power must be made up by (a) creating purchasing-power additional to domestic Wages and exporting it abroad as loans and investments or by (b) creating it for capital investment at home. Alternatively—that is to say, in the absence of both Foreign Investment and Domestic Capital expenditure—the systematic deficiency of purchasing-power will show itself as increasing impoverishment by "economy" and unemployment, and, in the end, in a crisis which, in effect, is a breakdown. In the case of the breakdown in America, for example, it is true that it was the cessation of the policy of Foreign lending that precipitated the crash; the insufficiency of domestic purchasing-power was no longer supplemented by the creation for export of purchasing-power to be used in the American market by foreigners. But it is not true that the cessation of foreign lending was the fundamental cause of the crash, since the very policy of foreign lending itself was the consequence of and was made possible by a deficiency of domestic purchasing-power inherent in the existing Monetary system, and certain sooner or later to reveal itself n one form or another. It is true, again, that had America, when she ceased creating purchasing-power, additional to Wages, for export, created in its place corresponding milliards of purchasing-power for domestic use, the crash need never have occurred and the boom of 1929 might have been continued to this day (if desired); but it is obviously unthinkable, according to the canons of "sound" finance, that having ceased to create money to lend abroad because the debts were becoming unpayable, her bankers would then be disposed to create an equivalent amount of money to lend at home without any prospect of repayment either. Left thus without the supplement of either Purchasing-power specially created for export or Purchasing-power specially created for home use, the fundamental deficiency of purchasing-power arising from so-called natural causes began to reveal itself in all its immensity. For a while, the stores of saved purchasing-power will conceal the gaping defect. For a little longer, transfers of purchasing-power from citizen to citizen by charity and by taxation will also contribute to concealing the defect. But in the end and in the absence of (a) Foreign Investment, (b) Domestic Investment (and both without expectation of repayment), or (c) free gifts of specially created purchasing-power to consumers as such in the form, for example, of National Dividends—it is absolutely inevitable that the plight of America—again, as an example—will go from bad to worse.   II 22

The Cure of Crisis

We are for the nation's control of its own financial credit—which, incidentally, does *not* require the nationalization of the Banks. We are for the institution immediately, as both an act of justice and an emergency measure, of National Dividends, that is to say, of participating shares for every citizen in the flow of wealth of the community. And we are for the establishment of the Just Price, that is, for Price measured by net Cost. These conditions of economic nationalism fulfilled—and none of them requires the sanction of any foreign State whatever, or could not be put into legislation in a month—we believe that the world-situation in general would immediately begin to find its claws drawn. Tariffs, armaments and wars are, as everybody is privately aware, matters *not* of foreign trade in the honest sense of the exchange of complementary goods. Nor are they even the consequences of competition for legitimate trade. The claws in the world-situation to-day consist of financial credits, extracted by the price-system from every industrial nation by its Bankers, and utilized *en masse* for the purpose of creating creditor-debtor relations among the peoples to their mutual injury and hatred.   II 2

Credit for Consumption

The creation and distribution of Credit or Purchasing-power in aid of Consumption *as such* is, we agree, a hard pill to swallow. But it is difficult only in sentiment—not in theory or in practicability. Theoretically it is not only just that every citizen as a joint heir of the entailed estate of the community and, at need, an active partner and sufferer in its defence, should be granted a share in its fruits, but, on less natural if more realistic grounds, it is altogether impossible, if technology continues to develop, to ensure for more than a diminishing number employment in paid production.

Either what appears to be free and unearned provision for Consumption *as such* must be deliberately made by society—simultaneously and progressively with provision for Production, or Production itself will be brought to a standstill either by wholesale sabotage or by revolution. The pill of "Money for Nothing" may be bitter for old men of all ages to swallow, but the alternatives before society are to swallow it or perish. We assert with complete confidence that the acceptance and legislation of the principle of the National Dividend is absolutely essential to the mere maintenance and not only to the welfare of modern Civilization. It is a matter for modern nations of National Dividends or Death.

It is nothing less than disgraceful ignorance for people to object that the legislation of National Dividends or of the Just Price presents such practical difficulties that, however theoretically desirable, it is administratively non-viable. Consider one of the minor social services, that of the Post Office Savings Bank, with its nine and a half million depositors. This service, entailing millions of operations, is, as everybody knows, discharged with a maximum of efficiency in the spare time of a staff simultaneously discharging a hundred other complex duties. It has been objected again that the institution of National Dividends and of the Just Price would involve such an intolerable amount of official inspection and of official uniformity that, to all intents and purposes, the nation that adopted them would be indistinguishable from a Servile State. This threat, however, is losing its terror from mere familiarity with its progressive realization; and is, indeed, one of the chief incentives to the adoption of Social Credit as the only means of avoiding it. Once again it is a matter of choice for nations; to put Production in chains and Consumption with it, to the ultimately fatal disadvantage of both; or to free Consumption while leaving Production at least as free as it is at present. It is nonsense to contend that the freeing of Consumption presents greater administrative difficulties than the shackling of Production. Unheard of and incredible administrative regulations are now being imposed and accepted in the most individualistic state in the world as well as in the most "communist". One per cent of such regulations applied to Consumption would not only release Consumption but at the same time remove from Production the necessity for 99 per cent of them. And we may add, of our own knowledge, that administrative experts, with no axe to grind, are agreed with us that when any nation is ready to adopt Social Credit principles, their practicability can be guaranteed with considerably more confidence than the practicability of the anti-natural devices now being adopted even by President Roosevelt. III 18

What would be the use of "nationalizing" the Banks if, after nationalization, exactly the same "sound money" policy as now governs the Banks continues to be pursued? Not the administration, which is admirable, and not the equally admirable personnel of the existing Banks are, in fact, in any serious degree in question. The vital and only important question is one of policy—what do you want your Monetary system to do? Assuming that your object is identical with that of the existing authorities, namely, to maintain the

industrial system, not as a system for producing and distributing the maximum of the best goods and services, but as
an agency for the provision of disciplinary employment—
then there is no useful purpose served in "nationalizing" the
existing private financial mechanism. Mr. Montagu Norman cannot conceivably be bettered as the moral task-
master of a community condemned to penal servitude in the
midst of plenty. On the other hand, if, as President Roosevelt declares, with the agreement of all enlightened people,
the proper objective of a Monetary system is to enable the
community to enjoy the fruits of its own labour, constantly
increasing the one while reducing the other—then it will not
be enough for the State merely to reassert or even to "take
over" the existing private system, it must at the same time
direct policy to the new aim of instrumenting Consumption
by other means, if need be, than by requiring that "work"
shall be done for it, irrespective of its real economic service.

IV 15

To the ordinary common-sense mind, the conclusion
would appear to be that since our mechanical productive
resources have so developed that an increasing amount of
Goods can be produced with a diminishing amount of
human labour, the community that has thus triumphed over
Man's primeval curse could well afford a generous distribution of leisure at the expense of machinery.

II 10

The administration of a Money Monopoly may be good
or bad; and it may be good or bad equally when decentralized or centralized. But it is not the administration that is
responsible for the fundamental defects, chronic or even
occasional, of the Money-system as a whole; but the fact
that it is a monopoly. The proposals here advocated would

simply transfer and restore the existing financial control—
which is obviously effective—from its present private and
irresponsible monopolists to the nation. This transfer or restoration to the community of its sovereign rights over its
own money would not involve the nationalization of the
Banks or, in fact, the nationalization of anything else. The
capitalist system of Production for Profit which has been so
successful in stimulating invention could well and wisely be
continued. Private property in every sense in which it is a
human desire would equally remain untouched. Even the
wage-system could be continued until such time as the
national dividend had taken its place. On the other hand,
once in control of its Money, a nation could monetize its
productive resources to the full and, while conducting foreign trade by employing money as a medium of exchange,
employ money within its own territory as a means of distribution mainly. In short, the reform for which the world is
dying is the nationalization of money; and this is clearly
within the power, as it is unmistakably within the urgent
obligation, of a political democracy. It is this alone that can
transform a political into an economic democracy and ensure the world against a return to dictatorships—Fascist,
Communist, Technocratic or Samurai.   II 13

Economic Nationalism

  The era of Foreign Investment, that is, of International Moneylending, is over. The future is with reciprocal and complementary foreign trade in Goods and personal Services.

  The old "favourable balance of trade" theory is dead.
Henceforth there is only one criterion of a favourable
balance—that the advantages to both parties balance.

  National Budgets, based upon the taxation of individual

earnings, will prove progressively more and more difficult to balance as the Overheads of the State increase at the same rate at which the sum of individual earnings diminishes.

The Gold Standard has gone for ever.

There will never now be possible a Super-State or World-government based upon the concentrated monopoly of Money. The so-called World-plot has failed.

Unemployment is one of the permanent and increasing products of Machine Industry. There is and can be no cure for it. Its proper treatment is by the National Dividend; and its proper name is Leisure.

As the last hundred or so years have seen the development of political nationalism, the movement has already begun towards the completion of political nationalism in economic nationalism.

Every sovereign nation will tend to resume control over its own monetary system and to create a National Financial Credit Account in strict correspondence with its National Real Credit Account.

From this National Credit Account will be paid (a) all the State overheads now charged by taxation to individuals; and (b) National Dividends for all citizens, without distinction.   II 11

The Meaning of Money
        The flaw in the existing system is at bottom due to the fact that instead of Money being regarded as a medium of exchange extra-territorially and as simply a medium of distribution intra-territorially, the former function of Money as a medium of exchange has completely swallowed up its latter function as a medium of distribution; with the result that the contributory partners in industry—the nation at large, including each and all of its citizens—are regarded

by the Money-monopolists as being upon precisely the same footing in the matter of Price as people entirely outside the economic association. For consumers within the national association and for consumers outside the national association there must, however, be two entirely different functions for Money. As between independent national communities, the proper function of Money is to act as a medium for the exchange of values; but as regards the members of any given community itself, the proper function of Money is not to act as a medium of exchange, but as a means of distribution pure and simple. It follows from this that the "reforms" that are necessary are not in the sphere of technical production but in the sphere of Money. So long as the notion of Money as a medium for the exchange of goods (proper, we repeat, to economic relations between independent communities) is permitted to govern the economic relations between the members themselves of independent communities, so long will not only the existing system "fail to deliver the goods" where they are needed, but also every other system whether Communist, Fascist or Technocratic. A nation's Money is its sovereign means of disposing of its collective resources. By control of its Money-system the nation collectively can control both foreign exchange and domestic distribution. As the Banks, to which the Crown criminally pawned the nation's sovereign power over its own money, have discovered, it is not in the least degree essential to effective control to be in possession, still less in administration, of the material resources of the nation. Anybody can "own" industry, anybody can administer industry; the final control is still with Money.   II 13

Briefly
      The National Income, in the form of Wages, Salaries

F

and Profits, has never been sufficient and will be increasingly insufficient, as the use of solar energy is extended, to purchase the annual national Production at Cost. It follows from this that it is not possible by any mere redistribution of Income to affect the economic situation fundamentally. And Labour's insistence upon the further taxation of the other classes will provoke the reaction called Fascism.

The very possibility of economic Employment is diminishing proportionately with the increase in the efficiency of Power Production. It follows from this that not only must Employment decline in value as a means of distributing purchasing power, but the factor of Labour in Production must continuously diminish in importance. As economic power precedes and conditions political power, the political power of Labour is a vanishing quantity.

The investment abroad of the domestically undistributed and constantly increasing surplus of Production over Consumption is no longer possible as a safety-valve. There are no longer "credit-worthy" countries. £62 millions even of the League of Nations' loans of £66 millions are in default. It follows from this that Labour can never hope again to find Employment and Wages from the export of Capital.

III 25

That there should be no doubt in any future Statesman's mind of the means necessary to the fulfilment of his presumed aim of levelling up Consumption to Production, we will set down the propositions upon which his policy must rest. They are as follows:

(1) The fact that the problem has arisen at all is ample evidence that the processes of Production do not automatically create and distribute sufficient purchasing power to absorb the total Production.

(2) The gap thus produced between the total costs (and therefore collective price) of this Production and the purchasing power distributed in the process, is both inherent in the present financial system, and tends to increase as Power displaces human labour.

(3) This gap has been hitherto at least partially bridged by the deliberate creation and distribution of additional purchasing power by (a) export credits or foreign investment, and (b) bank-credits for capital production, both productive and non-productive.

(4) With the slowing down and cessation of these, from any cause, the gap in question begins to yawn more and more widely; signs of it multiply on all sides in the form of increasing unemployment, bankruptcies; in short, in the social phenomena now everywhere visible, including the ideological "movements" called Communism and Fascism.

(5) To close the revealed and ever-widening gap, two schools of practical thought make their appearance: one, the orthodox school, whose only suggestion is to resume foreign investment and capital production as quickly and as lavishly as possible; and, the other, the Social Credit School, whose suggestion it is to create and distribute the necessary purchasing-power *not* through the processes of Production for either foreign investment or for superfluous domestic capital Production, but simply and solely for the purpose of Consumption.

(6) Apart from the facts that the resumption of foreign investment on an effective scale is now and for ever impossible, and that capital Production for reproductive purposes only widens the said gap, the attempt to increase Consumption through Production is not only doomed to fail but doomed, in its course, to destroy Productive initiative.

(7) On the other hand, the policy of instrumenting

domestic Consumption directly, and without the inter-
mediaries of Production for Export or superfluous Public
Works, would not only immediately begin to work, but
in its application it would involve not more and more but
less and less State interference with Production.   IV 2

The chart offered in his evidence before the Macmillan
Commission by Major Douglas to illustrate the close relationship between bankruptcies and suicides was rejected from
the final printed Report and, no doubt, for good reasons.
From the returns of the Registrar-General, however, it
appears that, like the good work of birth-control by murder,
the good work of death-control by suicide is still going on,
and at a rate still, we believe, in close correspondence with
the progressive restriction of Consumption by the Bank of
England. For the year 1932 the rate of suicide was the highest ever recorded, being at 143 per million, 14 per million in
excess of the previous record of 129 per million in 1931.
Close upon six thousand suicides occurred in England in
1932—some 100 or so every week—and by means in this
order of hatred of life—gas, drowning, hanging and poison-
ing. Lord Morley used to say that in his judgment, England
was a paradise for the rich, a purgatory for the able, and a
hell for the poor. But since his day and with the help of the
financial authorities, we have improved in diabolism upon
this, the fact being that today the whole threefold structure is
sinking deeper and deeper into the pit, the poor becoming
more unhappy, the able more despairing, and even the rich
more frequently snake-bitten in their orchid-house. It is
mocking at suffering and the Decline and Fall of a great
people to profess, as our statesmen do, that the clouds are
lifting, or that prosperity is round the corner. The clouds are
still gathering; and there is at present no direction of thought

in the most powerful quarters even to promise a permanent prosperity. One hundred suicides a week is already an indictment of the existing system more eloquent and appealing than any words. IV 11

Speaking at the opening of the new Mersey Tunnel, the [late] King first referred to the miracle of its creation. "Who can reflect upon it", he asked, "without awe at the will and power of man?" And then he went on to say that such an undertaking is not the labour of individual men but of many; and could only be achieved by "the endeavours of a multitude". But even "multitude" is, in our humble opinion, an unjustified restriction upon the number of people indispensable to "such an enterprise"; nor is an enterprise even on the scale of the Mersey Tunnel the only undertaking to call for the co-operation of all. Behind the "multitude" of the actual craftsmen all over the country engaged, directly or indirectly, in the technical construction of the Tunnel, was the vaster multitude of the whole nation, with its history, its heritage, its traditions, its character. As truly as it can be said that a nation conducts a war, even though only its professional troops may actually be engaged in it, the nation of England is the creator of the Mersey Tunnel, though only a multitude of technicians have been actually engaged in it. Nor, as we have suggested, is the national creative ability manifested only in works on a grand scale. In the production of everything, from a Mersey Tunnel to a pin, from a Cathedral to a child's go-cart, the nation at large is by far the major producing partner. Without the nation, even the most resourceful individual would have no more productive ability than a Robinson Crusoe; and most of our captains of industry would die of want. The conclusion from this undeniable fact points unmistakably to the justice of a

National Dividend. If it can be said that their Wages, Salaries and Profits constitute the just payment of the individuals directly employed, there is still, for the nation at large, the question of its share as the superior partner—though not in the Wages paid its working partners, but in the fruits of the common national enterprise. And perhaps the King had this in mind when he concluded his address with the wish: "May our people always work together thus for the blessing of this kingdom by wise and noble use of the power that man has won from nature." V 15

MONETARY THEORY

Laws in Economics

A system in economics is like a machine in mechanics; once constructed it runs by its own laws.   IV 12

In economics, it must be remembered, there are conventions as well as laws, conventions being man-made and laws being according to unalterable nature. Economic conventions can therefore be changed, while economic laws have only to be obeyed. The progressive diminution of returns for a uniform application of energy, for example, is an economic law. On the other hand, the Gold Standard, for instance, is only a man-made convention. The vast majority of the so-called "economic laws" under which we exist without living are, in fact, only conventions at bottom, rules of the game established not by Nature but by men themselves. Once, however, that a convention is established, the sequence of events arising from it is strictly and therefore calculably according to law. You arrange, by convention, a set of rules for a game, and to the degree that the game is strictly played, the consequences are predictable—statistically if not in every individual case. The Bank at any Casino, for example, must always win in the long run, just as loaded dice will always take the pool eventually. To cut the story short, it is equally inevitable that, given the economic conventions established and existing today, economic law will ensure precisely all the phenomena of the prevailing Depression, be the actors who they may. The question to be asked of any professed economic reformer is therefore this: "Have you changed any of the *conventions* of the game? Is the fundamental *system* in any essential respect new?

It is plain that, hitherto, the major conventions of the economic game have been (a) the commissioned Monopoly of Money by groups of private individuals; (b) their regulation of the supply of Money by relation with some other standard than that of economic Production; (c) the creation and appearance of all Money as debt ultimately to a bank; (d) the accounting of all Depreciation or Costs into Price without any deduction or allowance for the concurrent Appreciation; (e) the distribution of purchasing-power, that is, the right to participate in the communal wealth, conditionally upon direct participation in Industry alone; and (f) all State expenditure must be a charge upon individuals.

III 16

Money and Barter

Barter is the end-result of every series of exchange, but, from the days when money entered the picture, the simple single process implied in barter has been enlarged by the addition of monetary links until the chain that separates Goods from Goods is now as long as International Finance. In the first instance, the Goods are not exchanged immediately for Goods but for Money. In the second instance, the Money received for the Goods is again exchanged immediately not for Goods but for still other Money. And only finally, when these intermediate monetary processes have taken place, is the "barter" of the original Goods actually completed. Will anyone assert that the repeated intervention of a monetary carrier between Goods and Goods leaves the act of barter in its primitive state of innocence? Is there no jiggery-pokery possible and probable in the passes and sleights that affect and sophisticate the simple exchange? And when it is remembered that practically no trade today is barter, but every exchange must pay toll for a monetary carrier, insufficient in amount, monopolist in ownership and rack-renting in control, it will be clearly understood why the world must eliminate the "jiggery-pokery" from the existing money-system.   I I

Money and Metal
· To a certain degree, the subject of Money is no longer quite the holy mystery it was. Even the blindest devotees at the shrine of Gold have begun to suspect the motives of a high priesthood, not one of whose number has suffered when all the rest of the world has suffered. At the same time, it is evident that a monetary medium is a necessity of civilization and that confidence in its universal acceptability is a condition of its efficiency. With the dethronement of Gold, what is to succeed it? Here again we have the temerity to say that the answer is simple and that it is known. In the end this is a matter of psychology, and chiefly the realization of certain facts, hard, we agree, for people to realize whose experience for millennia has been of slavery to the parsimony of Nature and competition for the lion's share at a precarious table. The most important fact is that there is, now available, abundance for all.   I I

Nevertheless, there are still old ladies about—often disguised as experts as well as "practical men"—who cling to the notion that money is not real unless it is metallic—in spite of the fact that in no circumstances are they ever likely to see a gold sovereign again. And there are still more people about who, for the moment, are incapable of conceiving a currency based directly instead of indirectly upon the Real

Credit, namely, the actual ability of a community to deliver Goods and Services when, where and as required. It will take them some time, moreover, and not a little honest thought to realize that, in fact, the Gold of the Money-monopolists has never had and never can have more than its own intrinsic value as one of the inferior metals; and that its symbolic value, as one of the materials used in Money-manufacture, is, in the first place, the purely arbitrary creation of its ring of owners (whose predecessors similarly treated cowries, copper-wire and a host of other things); and, in the second place, is ultimately dependent upon what there is to buy, that is to say, upon precisely the state of the communal Real Credit. On the other hand, since not only the need to understand it is imperative, but the occasion is likely to demand it, we believe that even these people, even the man in the street, will before long realize that it is just as easy and far more advantageous to everybody but the Gold monopolists to base a currency upon Production directly than upon Production indirectly through the arbitrary agency of Gold. The last arguments for the Gold Standard that it automatically regulates internal currencies (thus preventing undue Inflation or undue Deflation) and at the same time automatically regulates International Exchange, have no longer a leg left to stand on. The worst can happen equally to countries on Gold and off Gold; and wars, it has not been observed, are impossible among nations on the Gold Standard. In short, both Gold and the Gold Standard are in respect of Monetary Science as obsolete as the Philosopher's Stone in respect of Chemistry. Our children will laugh at us for ever having believed in it and, above all, in the charlatans who have traded in it and on their simple parents.

It remains to be said, however, that though the Gold Standard is irreparably discredited for intelligence, its beneficiaries are unlikely to surrender their monopoly without a final struggle. The law of Reason, we know, is all-powerful in the long run, but in the short run of a mere generation or so, the possession of power is nine points of the law, even against reason. III 12

Speaking in his own county of Yorkshire, the Earl of Harewood, the son-in-law of the [late] King and Queen, expressed himself as having always wanted to ask the expert bankers why it is they insist on the importance of the Gold Standard. It appeared to him, on the contrary, as to every plain man undazzled by authority and propaganda, that "if all the Gold now at the Bank of England were transferred to Loch Ness to the care of that other monster"—the difference to the real wealth of the nation would be inappreciable. It is true that the noble Earl went on to say that the difficulty lay in finding another basis for Money in place of the metal Gold—as if, as is probable, he had never been allowed to hear of one—but it is also true that to a mind that has once perceived the stupendous absurdity of the Gold Standard, the understanding of the Production-Consumption standard would present no difficulties. Critics of the theories of Social Credit are often under the impression that they fail to understand them on account of their difficulty or because their exponents are obscure or at variance or over-technical. But the truth of the matter is that, in the majority of cases of dissent, the cause is to be found either in failure to understand the existing system of Finance or in the short-sighted instinct of immediate self-preservation. IV 14

The reason, the Earl of Harewood will be interested to know, for the fanatical attachment of the bankers to the Gold Standard is that by professing to be compelled to regulate the quantity of their loan-credits by the amount of Gold they have in their vaults, they can claim to be automatically and not merely arbitrarily limited in their use of the national credit. It is true that, in actual practice, the limits placed on their loans are not determined by their Gold-holding; for if this were the case the total money in existence at any given moment would be simply a multiple of the Gold. On the other hand, it is extremely convenient to employ a standard that at one and the same time gives the Banks both power to inflate the currency to any extent they choose, and power to insist upon its deflation in the name of sound finance. No other "standard" could conceivably be so elastic to the demands of bankers for Inflation or Deflation just when either of these suited them. If loan-credits were limited by an Index, or were subject to control by the relation of national Production to national Consumption, the bankers would lose their present power of "fixing the volume of credit", and therewith their present absolute control over the nation's life. The quantity of money in circulation would no longer be susceptible of their own determination by pretended reference to Gold, but it would begin to be regulated by the facts that in any case alone give Money its reality—the ability of the community to produce Goods and Services. There is no wonder, it will be seen, that bankers cling to the Gold Standard. IV 16

The Government, while loudly professing to be "off the Gold Standard", makes every effort to remain on it. Before the Government officially "went off" Gold, after having tried in vain to remain on it, sterling was "pegged" at 113 grams of gold to the £. At the present time, when we are officially "off Gold", sterling is still "pegged" to Gold, by means of the Exchange Equalization Fund, only at 85 instead of at 113 grams to the £. What does it matter, however, whether the £ is "pegged" at one figure or another to Gold so long as it is "pegged" to Gold at all? Except for the effects of the difference between 85 and 113 grams to the £ the monetary system of this country is as completely "on Gold" to-day as it was before it went "off Gold". It is true that there are fluctuations round about the "parity" of 85 to the £ exactly as there were round about the parity of 113 to the £, but as the means of checking them, namely, the issue and cancellation of credit by the Bank of England, are precisely the same as they were, the difference between being on and off Gold is a difference without distinction. Professor Cannan attributes the equivocal policy of the Treasury to its "Gold Mentality", its inability after years of use to think in other terms than Gold. We ourselves, however, would seek another explanation. It is not the case, we believe, that the Treasury officials are unable to think of money without seeing Gold. If they are as senile as that it is time to superannuate them. But it is, we believe, the case that the Bank of England will not let them.   I 10

To procure a fair verdict against the Gold Standard or Foreign Lending is just as difficult in this country as in the Southern States it is difficult to procure a verdict against a white man accused of injustice against a negro. Every jury is packed, and not by bribery alone, but by prejudice and the Gold superstition. On the face of it, nobody would conceive it possible to institute and maintain a system (a) that automatically restricts the spending-power of a nation, no matter what its real resources, to a multiple of the number of ounces of a useless metal it can obtain, and (b) that reckons its prosperity in terms of the quantity of its unpaid exports. Nevertheless, such is the savagery of the prevalent superstition that not only is reason lost on the Gold cult, but its critics are regarded as lunatics or, in Professor Keynes's phrase, victims of pathology. Against such superstition it is hard to struggle; and Mr. Leigh puts the situation neatly when he says that "it is as if the London Chamber were explaining a motor car and the critic felt he had successfully disposed of the possibility of such a thing working, first, by showing that there were no reins; secondly, that in that case it would be impossible to steer the horses; and, thirdly, that if motor cars were to supersede quadrupeds, there would be a scarcity of manure". Psycho-analysis might suggest that the last argument is usually decisive.   V 6

Money owes its value simply and solely to the total productive resources of a community and to the consent of the citizens to honour it—in a word, to a community's Real Credit. The metal Gold has only a small share in the total Production, and even with the addition of Silver, the so-called precious metals play only an insignificant role in the real economics of a community. And to single out one or even two of these, and to insist that the community shall restrict its Consumption of its total Production merely to a multiple of the number of ounces of Gold and Silver it happens to have, is about as sensible as starving at a banquet because you haven't a platinum fork.   V 17

A sufficient reply to the proposal to monetize Silver is that you do not alter the present distributive forces by merely increasing the amounts of money at their disposal. Loaded dice do not become unloaded by multiplying the stakes. If it is true, as it is, that, thanks to the play of existing forces, America and France have now most of the Gold of the world, there is nothing in the long run to prevent them getting all the Silver in the world as well, and, above all, if Gold is retained as the superior token of financial value. Again, as America has surely proved to the world, there is no use in simply adding to the quantity of the money, in currency or credit, available in the Bank reserves for borrowing if there is nobody who dare borrow for fear of finding no customers. Money at the factory—that is, the Bank—may be as cheap and plentiful as the cotton-goods of the Lancashire mills, but if there is nobody to use it, the more there is of it the more obviously useless it becomes. I II

The truth of the matter is that you cannot make people borrow merely by making money cheap, unless they can also be assured of a profitable market for the product of their loans. Without denying any advantage whatever in cheap or plentiful money (money as a commodity, of course, not money as purchasing power), we can safely say that the reduction in the price of money from seven to three per cent or even to no "interest" at all, would have very little if any effect upon business today. It is not the interest or the price of the loan that matters nowadays, it is the loan itself and the difficulty, not to say the impossibility, of repaying it. The reason for this, again, has little to do with either Deflation or Inflation taken by themselves. Inflation and Deflation are merely the alternating currents employed by Banks of Issue to maintain their control over their three monopolistic privileges—the regulation of the issue of money to producers, the regulation of its recovery by means of prices from the consumer, and the control of its distribution among both by taxation. It is a mistake, therefore, to think that Central Banks arbitrarily favour Deflation or arbitrarily oppose Inflation. Their only arbitrariness is in their paramount monopoly of the control they exercise over the very life-blood of economic society; since with the heart of Industry in their hands they can employ the systole and diastole of Inflation and Deflation to bloat or bleed their victims into complete subjection. The only remedy we know against this is the National control of credit; the free distribution of credit to authorized producers; the free distribution of the product to authorized consumers. Without such a "drastic" and "audacious" reform it is inevitable that, like civilizations before ours, faced with the same monetary problem and without the intelligence and will to solve it—Rome being the classic example—ours will rot and fall and the world will return to the Dark Ages.   I 5

That the limits of man's use of his own created wealth should have been allowed for so long to be arbitrarily fixed by the quantity of Gold in his possession is a bitter reflection on human intelligence, but it is encouraging to note that not only are our publicists now ready to go off and to keep off Gold, but that they have begun—tentatively, it is true—to examine the possible alternatives to the Gold Standard. The first device, naturally, that has come to their mind is to expand the "fiduciary issue", that is to say, to add to the State-guaranteed securities, now amounting to £275 millions, which constitute the ultimate "currency" resources for the issue of bank-credit by the Bank of England. As at present "managed" (for, of course, our financial system has always been a "managed" one), the "fiduciary issue" (in reality, the Government's standing debt to the Bank) has been liable to be supplemented by the Bank's holding of Gold. The possible legal tender, which is the basis upon which banks issue credit in the form of purchases, loans and overdrafts, has thus been hitherto composed of the fixed sum of the "fiduciary issue" *plus* the variable sum of the gold holding of the Bank.

If we are now to go off Gold for good, and to accumulate no more of it in the Bank as a supplementary basis for the issue of Credit, it is obvious that unless we are prepared for further deflation, either the "fiduciary issue" must be increased to make up for the permanently absent gold, or some new basis for financial credit must be invented or found. We can well understand the doubts and fears that must assail the adventurer into these new and untrodden ways. Upon leaving what until recently has appeared to him to be the solid ground of a gold backing for his "money" (although, in reality, there has never been any such "backing", as the recurrent suspensions of the Bank Act might have revealed to him), he naturally feels nervous when, as it seems, he is invited to walk henceforward on air. And equally naturally his first disposition is to get as near to the old familiar "standard" as possible, and, in the absence of Gold, to rest his whole weight on the other support, namely, the "fiduciary issue" and to increase that. In fact, however, as he will soon discover, the "fiduciary issue" is not only even more shadowy than the shadowy Gold backing that is now to vanish completely, but it must stand in quite as arbitrary and imperfect a relation with actual economics as ever Gold did. There is, indeed, in the long run, no other practical alternative to Gold as the basis of Financial Credit than the Real Credit of the nation, defined by Major Douglas in simple yet accurate terms, as the ability of the community to produce and deliver Goods and Services as, when and where required. With our providentially enforced abandonment of the Gold Standard, it is now possible that England may find salvation first, and not last, of the nations. For by creating a financial system that shall reflect in terms of Money the actual facts of our Productive System, instead of vice versa, we shall not only have at last a truly sane Money-

G

sytem, but therewith the key to our own and the world's prosperity. II 8

Even in the most "expert" circles, it is well known that the proper functioning of the Gold Standard presupposes if not the actual possession of gold, at least the access to gold; and it is equally a fact beyond dispute that at the present moment the bulk of the gold of the world is securely buried in the vaults of the American and French Central Banks. Now how, we ask, is this gold to be released? How is the rest of the world to obtain its use for the proper functioning of the Gold Standard? There are, as everybody ought to know, two ways and two ways only of prying open the safes of the American and French Central Banks: (a) by persuading America or France to import goods from the rest of the world in such excess of her exports that the difference in values payable in gold begins to deplete her stores of the metal; and (b) by persuading either or both countries to make foreign loans of credit on a colossal scale. But to anybody acquainted with the conditions and psychology of both the French and the American peoples, it is simply ridiculous to expect of either the adoption of either means. And if neither America nor France will "play the game", it follows that the silly game cannot be played by the rest of the world. In fact, the reign of Gold is over. II 4

Money and Industry
To any unprejudiced mind, the functions of the Industrial and Financial mechanisms of any given community are perfectly clear. Industry exists to produce and deliver where required the maximum of the best possible goods in the best possible way; and Finance exists to facilitate the same by accurate book-keeping. It is a truism that the only value of

Money is as a representative of Goods; but it is unfortunately less commonly agreed that the only value of Industry is to provide Goods. The making of Money (though, in truth, nobody makes Money except the Banks) or the provision of Employment—these and not simply the production and distribution of useful Goods, are taken to be the proper objective of Industry, with the result that not only are useful Goods in short supply, but, as a natural penalty, Industry itself fails both to "make money" and to "provide employment". In view of the breakdown of our industrial Civilization—that is to say, of a Civilization in which sovereign policy has been allowed to be defined by the essentially subordinate functions of Industry and Finance—some new and clear affirmation of national policy in respect of both Industry and Finance is tragically urgent. It may be, as Fascists and Communists alike believe, that statesmen have become too deeply imbued with economic ideas to be able to reassert their own sovereignty. If that should prove to be the case, dictatorships of the Fascist or Communist type are inevitable. 16

Money and Credit

There is a hole, as inexhaustible as our national Real Credit, from which money can be taken and from which money is taken—but by the banks at present only. Whenever in fact, the Banks buy Treasury bills, or securities of any kind, or make a loan, or allow an overdraft, they draw the money, not from the pockets or accounts of their stockholders or depositors, but from a "hole in the ground" called their reserve or margin, but consisting, actually, of the reserve resources of the Productive capacity of the community. They literally, in short, manufacture money with which to enable their clients to "demand" the use of the nation's resources. If the private corporations called Banks can at will call up money from the vasty deep, and it comes, as it does, at call, there is no conceivable reason why the community itself should not do the same in their place. Exactly as bank loans and purchases are made without calling upon existing depositors to contribute to them (nobody's private account being diminished by the loans or purchases made by the Bank) the State, if it were in control of the hole, would be able to finance its services without directly calling upon the income of its citizens. All that would happen would be that the State and not the Banks would be the author of the consequent inflation, but that the inflation in the case of the State, would be the only form that taxation would take.   IV 25

Bank of England one-pound notes cost 5s. 6d. a thousand to produce.   II 23

The bankers have been pointing to the banking-deposits as evidence that there is no shortage of money in the country. Are these people really as stupid as they appear? Or are they paid to look it? A large percentage of the deposits represent simply securities bought by the banks at the expense of a book-entry entitling the banks to participate without risk in the enterprises of their hardy "customers". And however comparatively large the amounts of money lying unpiped in the deposit reservoirs, they are still only a fraction of the amount needed to monetize the real credit of the community. These petty tradesmen of high finance have a terror of any amount over the paltry millions of their Lombard great grandfathers. It gives them the same pain in the neck to see money expanded as was felt by the early fundamentalists as they saw Ussher's 4004 B.C. date for Creation expanding into the dark backward and abysm of time; they conceive no end to it; and, as the Gold Standard slips from under their feet they feel themselves to be hanging over a bottomless pit of "Inflation". On the optimistic assumption that, before long, the community will insist upon proper book-keeping and upon balancing its Budget in the only sensible way—that is to say, by recording in monetary tokens the real state of its economic affairs—it is certain, however, that the present figures of the banks will appear ludicrously small. The real credit of the community is not represented by a couple of thousand millions, but it would need an amount at least a hundred times as great to monetize it. With a quarter of a million million tokens to spend, each solidly representing a unit of real production, the community would at last be as rich in money as in goods. A thousand pounds a year per family would be well within the spending capacity of the nation both in terms of money and in terms of goods. Our bank ushers, however, will have to leave school before they dare to think in such amounts. At present they are compelling the community to live on its pocket-money. V 6

Credit for Production we do not, of course, deny is necessary. On the other hand, since the only *raison d'être* of Production is Consumption, unless the credits issued for Consumption keep pace with the issues of credit for Production, it is manifestly impossible not to ensure the existing condition of things—a Productive system gorged to vomiting with credit, and a Consumptive system starved to skin and bone with the denial of it. Until the rights of Consumption, as such, are as fully recognized, by the specific distribution of purchasing power which has not entered into Costs, as today the rights of Production are by the issues of credit entering properly into Costs, not even a beginning of a practical solution of the world's economic crisis is possible.

I 15

Money and Prices

Price-regulation today is not primarily concerned with the limitation of profits or even with the question of Costs. Costs and motives are for Producers; prices are for Consumers. Scientific price-regulation, as it will in all probability prevail before long, is concerned simply and solely with the ascertainment of the formula that will from time to time enable the nation effectively to demand all of the resources of its own Production that it cares to consume. Its sole purpose, in short, will be to transfer and distribute goods in an orderly and economic way.

IV 22

By a scientifically managed price-system, however, we do not mean what, unfortunately, is being now everywhere associated with the phrase, namely, the stabilization for all time of the internal purchasing-power of the dollar or pound or franc, in relation to the average price of a list of commodities, some eighty or so in number, in constant demand. As their average price varies, the Banks are to issue or cancel credit with the object of as nearly as possible keeping the purchasing power of the monetary unit stable. It is an imaginary remedy, however, for a purely imaginary disease. Not only is its application completely impracticable, but the effect of it, if it could be put into operation, would be to leave things very much as they are. It is true, no doubt, that the eighty or so articles selected for the Index are in constant demand; but it is also true that the maintenance of their average price is perfectly compatible with violent changes in their individual prices; and since there is no producer or

consumer who is equally concerned with all the commodities in the Index, the particular variations of price of his
own special commodities will continue to affect him precisely as they do now, in spite of the assurance that the average price of the whole eighty has been maintained. The
proposed reform, moreover, labours under another fatal
disadvantage, that of mistaking the disease for which it is
presumably prescribed. The economic disease of the age is
the inadequacy of the means of Consumption to the means
of Production, and that the root-cause of this discrepancy is
to be found in the failure of the Monetary system to distribute purchasing-power otherwise than as a function of
Production. What is the use, then, of merely stabilizing
prices (even supposing this to be possible) when, in fact, the
real problem is how to get more purchasing-power into
everybody's hands? Will it comfort the increasing army of
unemployed to be assured that a pound tomorrow will buy
the same amount of an average of eighty articles as it does
today? Will stabilizing average prices make the smallest
difference to the process of the substitution of natural for
human labour, and the consequent increasing disproportion
between Total Costs and Labour Wages?　　　II 20

Among the many objections that can be raised against the
proposal—even assuming that stabilization of prices is desirable in face of the development of Power-production and its
logical sequel in a progressive lowering of prices—there are
two that can and ought to be regarded as fatal.

The first objection is that the stabilization refers to an
average and not to any particular commodity included in
the "basket". Let it be agreed that the hundred or so commodities selected for the "basket" are fairly representative
of the purchases of the "average householder". Let it be

further agreed that, *if* there were such an actual being as an "average householder", his average purchases at the stabilized average could always be ensured by his averaged dollar unit. But the fact of the matter is that no such person as the hypothetic Mrs. 'Arris exists, either among the class of purchasers or among the class of producers. Economic experts with jobs in their bonnet have invented the game of weighted tables of commodities privileged to enter the charmed ring of their Index to qualify for average stabilization, but any actual consumer and any actual producer is certain to find himself at any and every given moment interested, not in the statistical average, but in those particular commodities in which in fact he is concerned, as consumer or producer. It is asserted in the unreal atmosphere of the classroom, that on the average the individual prices of the commodities selected for the basket "tend" to move in beautiful harmony, and that if not quite simultaneously their individual prices vary together within negligible periods of time. But a period of time negligible to an economic expert may be long enough to rob a householder and ruin a producer; and, apart even from this, the contention is literally without foundation. Only on an average, in short, do individual prices vary together, and only on an average, therefore, can either producer or consumer be satisfied with an average price.

The second objection is even more fundamental; and it applies with equal force to the proposal to stabilize the purchasing-power of the monetary unit and to all proposals that ignore or attempt to side-step the very problem for which nominally they profess to be solutions. That problem, we repeat, is the problem of increasing purchasing-power for the purposes of Consumption up to the limit of potential Production (not, we agree, all at once necessarily, but at any rate progressively). Let it be supposed, for example, that the present Plan for stabilizing average prices proves to be entirely successful. Let it be further supposed that, contrary to all probability, every individual producer and every individual consumer proves to be the complete embodiment of the fictitious "economic man". How much nearer are we brought even into effective touch with the original problem which is obviously only secondarily one of prices and primarily one of obtaining the monetary units with which to go shopping at all? There might be something (and even then not much) to be said for maintaining a constant monetary unit in terms of commodities, if the monetary units distributed over the whole community were sufficient to purchase the whole production of the community. If every man, woman and child in the community were in possession of the proportionate number of monetary tokens that collectively constituted an effective demand on the total national Production, a regulated Price-system would be desirable if only as a means of discovering the directions of Demand and the limits of Supply. But to propose to stabilize the purchasing power of the monetary unit *before* securing the distribution of a sufficient number of monetary units with which to purchase your Production is not only to incur all the disadvantages of an average that pleases nobody, but to leave untouched the original objective. It will be replied, no doubt, that the results to be hoped for from the stabilization of prices include the wider distribution of wages, the reduction if not the elimination of present indebtedness, and the increase of profits on an increased turnover. But apart from the fact that none of these results is probable, it is certain that even if they were, the root-problem itself would remain relatively unaffected. You can raise wage-rates and profit-rates all you please; but if, as undeniably is the case, the number of people employed or employable in Production is diminishing relatively to the increase in the mechanical means of Production, then the total pay-roll of the employed will not only be increasingly inadequate to demand the total Production, but even that pay-roll will have to be increasingly taxed, directly or indirectly, for the maintenance of the unemployed and unemployable. In other words, the higher wage-rates and profits will be in appearance only. They will go into the pockets of the employed, it is true, but mortgaged, as to an increasing fraction, for the maintenance of the unemployed. IV 3

The National Debt

Consider our National Debt of about eight thousand million pounds, the major part of which, as everybody knows, was incurred in the course of making the world safe for democracy. Since it represents—very feebly—the actual efforts and sacrifices as well as goods made and consumed during that period by the whole nation, and not merely by a small class alone, it is barbaric arithmetic, to say nothing of its morality, to saddle the burden of the debt on the whole nation while confining its repayment to a relatively few individuals. The debt itself, furthermore, if we look at it financially, was incurred on account of what may correctly be called National Capital Extension. England as a nation in business was called upon to meet a formidable competitor and was obliged to raise fresh capital in order to meet it; and this fresh capital, as we say, was subscribed in terms not only of money but of goods and services, and not only by the "City" but by every man, woman and child in the nation. Fortunately for this country—for we do not suppose there is even yet anybody in England who is not glad that Germany lost the war—the result was fairly satisfactory. Thanks to our Capital outlay, England emerged from the war at least temporarily disembarrassed of the competition of a threatening rival and in point of plant, skill and organization so well equipped that it is safe to say that our total productive ability had been increased by not much less than a hundred per cent. This increment of National Wealth, created, we cannot too often repeat, by the labour and sacrifices of the whole nation, is, if anything can truly be said to be, national property in which every individual is in justice an indisputable shareholder. Put its estimated value at the trifling sum it cost of eight thousand millions—it is obviously many multiples of that amount; and now apportion this estimated cost of the work expended on national Capital appreciation among the contributories, namely, the whole nation. The National Debt would thus be distributed to its rightful owners and every family in England entitled to an income from National Bonds of about £40 a year. If any "great statesman" is looking for a Monetary reform that is at once just, practical and remedial, here is one ready to hand. I 4

The Money Monopoly

It is all very well to say that if there were no tariffs, if there were no stock speculation, if foreign investment could always accelerate, the Monetary system of the fifteenth century could be made to work in the twentieth; but the Monetary system does not fail to work because of these things, but these things, on the contrary, are brought into existence because the system could not have lasted as long as it has without them. II 21

The international as well as the national traffic in Money is indubitably and in all senses the most profitable monopoly in the whole world, being, as it is, a monopoly that can and does control every other monopoly. Its power is almost beyond imagination. It is literally the truth that the heads of the Central Banks of the world, if they should agree, could determine the course of human society upon our whole planet. If the heads of nations do not know their business, the Money Monopolists at least know theirs; and in the absence of statesmen with intelligence and parliaments with responsibility it is perfectly certain that the Money-changers will continue to occupy and prostitute the Temple of civilization. 19

It is a platitude that unfortunately few people believe that Money is in itself nothing; that at best it is a convenient device for keeping track of Production and Distribution and that, at bottom, it is superfluous. In matters relating to Money the modern mind is in a state of complete savagery; and there is scarcely any "belief", however preposterous, that cannot and does not obtain currency in one tribe or another of "expert" medicine-men.

The experience of a good deal of controversy with "experts" as well as with amateurs convinces us that the principal cause of the tragical misunderstanding of Money is the inability to realize the possibility of carrying on Foreign Trade (it is always Foreign Trade, never the much more important department of Home distribution) without an internationally accepted medium, namely Gold. Unless your currency, so the argument runs, is linked with Gold, that is to say, has a fixed Gold value—it is impossible for two currencies to be easily exchanged one into the other; you can therefore never calculate exactly the relative prices of goods valued in a variety of currencies; and foreign trade, in consequence, would become chaotic. Now it is precisely this "argument for Gold" which Professor Cannan blows sky-high. Once again, if we may be allowed to say so, the old argument has been rendered unfit for intelligent company. Apart from the fact that the convertibility of national currencies into Gold has never secured international prices against fluctuations; apart, again, from the fact that Gold has long ceased to be only a token and has become itself the most valuable of commodities (as the raw material of bank-credit); and apart, finally, from the fact that no matter how much they try certain nations, willing and anxious to engage in world trade, either cannot get hold or keep hold of Gold with which to stabilize their domestic currencies internationally—apart, we say, from all these facts and not theories, the simple truth about the relative values of national currencies is that they exchange, with Gold or without Gold, *at their internal purchasing power*. To put it in the simplest possible form, the pound, the dollar, the mark and the franc exchange at values corresponding to what the pound will buy in England, the dollar in America, the mark in Germany or the franc in France. The fact is obvious when it is remembered that foreign exchanges are nothing more than exchanges of domestic currency; and domestic currencies, it is equally obvious, owe their value to what they will buy in their own market. As Professor Cannan says: "Theory and practice both teach that the long-run value of paper currencies depends not on budgets, balance of trade, nor on exchange speculation, but on their internal purchasing power." The internal purchasing power of national currencies, he says: "*can be regulated as easily as, or rather more easily than, that of any other monopolized commodity.*" This amounts to saying that you can make your national money, provided you have control of it, worth anything you please. The more you make it worth—that is to say, the more things it will buy—in your home market, the more the foreigner will pay for it when he comes shopping in your market, in other words, the higher your currency stands in terms of foreign exchange. We have only to suppose that the purchasing power of the £ were doubled in our domestic market, to the happy relief of the whole population, to see the £ in terms of every other country mounting to par and going to an unparalleled premium in terms of mere gold. And this doubling of our internal purchasing power is not only easily possible within the limits of our productive resources, but it can be effected without any other nation's "By Our Leave" or the possession of a gram of gold. I 10

Purchasing Power

Credits constitute a debt that has eventually to be paid back out of taxes (after having already in their issue directly taxed the community once!). It is obvious that, under the existing system of Costing and Pricing, every dollar of fresh credit put into Production, whether it actually increases Production or not, whether the Production is available for Consumption or not, whether it generates spendable incomes or not, is and must be debited to Cost and consequently to Price. Price, however, is, along with Money itself, one of the determinants of the power of purchasing, that is to say, of the effective means of Consumption. Money into Price is the measure of purchasing-power. Unless therefore the ratio of Money to Price is increased in favour of Money so that all the money, new and old, will actually buy more, the original proportion of purchasing-power to Production is either left unchanged or it is diminished. Since it is proposed, moreover, that certain new credits, though they are bound to create costs, which in turn must create prices, shall be spent, not upon consumable goods but upon capital goods (roads and warships), the

latter of which never come to market, it is obvious, again
to the simple child, that the price created by the new costs
arising from the new credits will be debited to consumable
goods exclusively, there being, in fact, no others upon which,
by their sale, the costs can be recovered. Condensing the
rest into a series of statements, all susceptible of rational
proof, and all likely to be demonstrated in practice, we can
say that the cost of living will rise proportionately with the
creation and issue of fresh credits for Production whether
of public or of private works; and that this constitutes an
indirect but effective tax on all fixed incomes; to the inevitable impoverishment of the professional classes. While
the "unemployed" are being absorbed, moreover, the demand for higher wages to meet rising prices will be relatively moderate; but as the policy of credits for Production
is continued and pursued, the demand will become more
insistent only to meet the increasing resistance of the suffering professional classes. In other words, the "class-war"
will begin to lift its ugly head. It will be impossible, on the
one hand, to prevent prices rising, since only by increased
prices can the cost of all Production be met; and if one tries
to regulate prices, the evasions will be wholesale. On the
other hand, it will be impossible to increase wages, since
not only would prices rise proportionately, but the rentier
class would decline to submit to total extinction. In these
circumstances, there are two alternatives, and two only: to
proceed to copy Stalin; or to find, not even to invent, a
means of increasing purchasing-power which does in fact
do what it sets out to do.   III 14

Deflation and Puritanism
     Professor Gustav Cassel has traced the craze for Defla-
tion (that is, for the destruction of productive activities of all

kinds) to the strain of Puritanism in industrial nations. Something was morally wrong when everybody was happy producing and consuming. Judgment was bound to fall upon the world, and the deflation was simply God's way of punishing man. Characteristically a Scottish banker, writing in the *Glasgow Evening Times* a criticism of Major Douglas's Plan for National Dividends, illustrates Professor Cassel's contention. Should Major Douglas's Plan really function, he says, "we should simply be inviting a repetition of the worst features of our post-war prosperity." And these worst features, it appears, were "lavish spending", insufficient saving, "reckless extravagance" and the earlier "retirement of a number of people from business". Without a scarcity complex aggravated by an unconscious Jah-veh-worship, it is impossible for anybody to regard as even bad features these typical and desirable symptoms of confident prosperity. There is not one of them to which all the world, saving flagellants, would not gladly return, and to which, moreover, return is not easily possible. Our most lavish spending and reckless extravagance certainly did not diminish our productive resources. As everybody knows, our productive resources increased rather than diminished as a result of the increased demand made upon them. The earlier retirement of people from business is a proper objective both for the individual and for the community. Retirement at thirty-five for a life of strenuous leisure would in all probability assure us an adult population worthy the respect and emulation of the young—without which all education is worse than useless. And as regards Saving, and most emphatically Saving for investment in production, it can be demonstrated that the Investment of Savings in production is one of the causes of the disparity between purchasing-power and costs. As the Dark Ages that put their surplus spending-power

into non-productive public works such as cathedrals instinctively realized, you cannot and must not try to drive
the mill with the water that has passed. I 8

Industrial Costs and Purchasing-Power

Everbody is aware that a characteristic feature of
the modern industrial system is the relative increase of
"Overheads" as compared with the sums disbursed in
Wages collectively. The cost of the maintenance and improvement of the capital plant of modern industry is increasing at a greater rate than the cost of direct labour:
which is to say that the total price value at cost of modern
production is constantly diminishing in respect of payments
to personnel—whether workers or shareholders. This ever-
widening disparity between "Overheads", represented
chiefly by bank-credits, and direct Labour-costs, which in
general constitute the sole source of actual purchasing-power,
would, in fact, long ago have proved fatal to society unless
it had been partially corrected by various devices; but quite
inevitably it cannot be corrected by tinkering for ever. The
time must come, and has come, when the sums disbursed
to individuals in industry will be patently insufficient to
discharge the Overhead costs plus the cost of living. And if
this is the case with Industry itself, and in the absence of
any other charge upon it, what must be the case when, in
addition to the Overheads of Industry proper, the Overheads of the State are charged to the same account? If the
individual consumer, from his individual income, must pay,
in price or taxation, the double burden of the Overheads
of Industry and the Overheads of the State; and if, furthermore, it is inevitable, as plant develops, that the recipients
even of direct labour costs will diminish in number, the
logical conclusion to be drawn is that an increasing burden

of both taxation and industrial Overheads will be laid upon a diminishing number of recipients of wages and salaries.

The ever-widening gap between the annually distributed purchasing-power (in the form of Wages, Salaries, Dividends and Profits; in sum, the monetary income of the community) and the selling-price of the year's production is a result, not of one or all of the causes to which it usually ascribed, but of the arithmetical fact that the selling-price of production, under our existing monetary and accountancy system, debits the purchaser—quite properly—with true cost, namely, Consumption, but fails to credit him simultaneously with the resultant Production. Let us suppose that the pomophagous workers in an apple orchard were charged each season for their year's supply of apples not *only* with the cost of the apples they consumed, but, in addition, with the cost of the maintenance and extension of the orchard, and also of the apples that fell and rotted on the ground, how long, we ask, would it be before the apples they could purchase would be more than a trivial fraction of the potential yield of the orchard? And if we add the circumstance that fewer and fewer workers were required, the parallel of their accursed Garden of Eden and the modern industrial world would begin to appear threateningly close. There is, we truly believe, no more potent cause of all our present economic miseries than this one simple fact, that the sum of the annual monetary incomes of any modern industrial community is increasingly insufficient to purchase the annual production at Cost as now reckoned. Unless, therefore, something is done about this growing gulf between purchasing-power and selling-prices—a phenomenon, we repeat, common to every modern community, irrespective of size, character, natural advantages, debts, tariffs, wars or birth-control—there is literally no use in anything else. Our pun-

dits, idealist or practical, may talk themselves black in the
face about their various propagandas. They will effect no
radical change in the absence of measures designed to increase distributed purchasing-power (in plain words, individual monetary incomes for spending) *pro rata* with the
increase of productive capacity.   II 9

Managed Currency

The common objection to a "managed currency"
is an example of the effect of propaganda, since, as anybody
can know who will give a moment to the supreme topic
of the age, every currency, private or State, is "managed",
the currency controlled by the Bank of England no less
than the currency controlled by the Soviet Government.
It is all a question of who it is that should manage it, and
we have very little doubt that in the opinion of the Bank of
England the answer is themselves. On the other hand, there
is equally no doubt in our minds or in the minds of any
plain citizen, that the duty of "managing" the currency is
a sovereign privilege of a sovereign people, and that any
delegation of a privilege, second only to kingship in rank
and power in a State, is an act of folly on the part of a
king's representative parliament and its complete submis-
sion to a non-elected, irresponsible private corporation not
far short of treason. The arraignment of a Treasury on a
charge of treason has been known in history before.   I 2

It is amusing to observe the change of fashion in Monetary
reform. One phrase holds the stage for a week or month or
two, to be succeeded by another and then another until
the turn of the first comes round again. Those with a memory
longer than a daily paper can recall, as it were but yesterday,
the craze for the return to Gold to enable the pound to look

the dollar in the face. After a very brief experience of the effect of this Gorgon glance, the cry went up for the extension of Industrial credits, in other words, for Inflation. Then came the tidal wave for the saving of the pound followed by the ebb in the form of panic-stricken warnings against the perils of Inflation once we were off the Gold Standard. The *dernier cri* is of none of these things, but of the creation of a sterling area within which the pound takes the place of gold as the standard of monetary value. And this will no doubt give way to still another cry—in all probability to one with which we are already familiar. What does it all mean, this chasing our own tails, this boxing of the compass? With the best will in the world to believe that it indicates serious thought about the supreme topic of the age, we find it impossible. The eternal recurrence of the stage army of slogans is unwelcome but convincing evidence that all our "experts" are continuing to think in the old grooves and only ringing the changes on the old, old misconceptions both of Money and of Industry. I 5

INDUSTRY AND AGRICULTURE

Production and Finance

It was Heraclitus who said that the simplest truths escape realization by their incredibility; and the wisdom of his remark is illustrated by the failure of the majority of our intelligent contemporaries to realize the relation between the Industrial and the Financial systems. Because the Financial system appears to depend upon the Industrial system for its meaning and even for its existence, it is assumed and accepted that it is somehow or other the reflection and servant of the Industrial system; whereas, in fact, the relation of the Financial to the Industrial system is that of ivy to an oak, it flourishes at the expense of its host. There are a multitude of evidences of this fundamental parasitism, the simplest, perhaps, being the patent and published contrast between the profits of the Banks and the losses of Industry; but it takes a little more perception and a little more open-mindedness to realize, even inadequately, the degree to which already the Money monopoly is in complete strangle-control of its Industrial victim. In some recent statistics prepared for the American Senate, it has been demonstrated with chapter and verse that by means of "interlocking directorates and financial intimidation", a few New York banks and bankers exercise a life and death control (that is to say, prosperity or bankruptcy) over nearly a thousand of the largest industrial corporations of America. With nothing else to play with than the counters of legal tender (which, in fact, constitutes their monopoly) and with no

117

other aptitude than cunning figuring, these few individuals manage to control and to have the beneficiary use of all the inventions of the whole of society and, in consequence, of society itself.   II 19

The fundamental facts of the world's production system today are the following:

(1) The old distinction between agricultural and manufacturing communities is no longer valid.

(2) Both machinery and power are today susceptible of practically worldwide distribution.

(3) Machine technique, as regards both operation and direction, is no longer subject to geographical or racial monopoly, artificial or natural.

(4) Domestic Unemployment is a universal problem; and so long as its solution is idiotically sought in More Employment, every community must aim at protecting its Home-market while at the same time attacking the Foreign Market; in short, at the maximum of Employment for its own people, and the minimum of Employment for foreigners.

(5) The international transfers of capital, taking the form of international debts, that formerly employed shipping under the control of the lending nations, are unlikely to be resumed. Few nations are now "credit-worthy"; and such as are will in future prefer to finance themselves.

(6) The War simultaneously taught neutral nations the precariousness of a policy that left many of them at the mercy of belligerents; and belligerent nations the precariousness of a policy that left many of them dependent upon neutrals—or even upon enemies. It is to be expected that not until an era of World Peace has been securely established

will any nation that can help it again risk laying its precious eggs in foreign baskets.   IV 20

Agriculture

The policy pursued by this country, ever since the Industrial Revolution, has been to accumulate foreign investments, instrumented by manufactured exports, and to import in partial exchange cheap foodstuffs for the maintenance of the working-classes: to make England in short, the workshop of the world, for the benefit of the "City" bondholders, and debtor nations the main and ultimately sole source of England's food. The most "drastic and far-reaching measures" of the Minister for Agriculture can obviously interpose, at best, only a minor impediment to the pursuit of this aim, if they are confined, as they are likely to be, to measures affecting agriculture alone. No amount of rationalization, new forms of marketing, scientific farming, change of ownership or even (single-taxers should note) remission of rents [in Norfolk, farms are a-begging rent free] will more than slightly affect the existing and increasing disproportion between Agriculture and Industry in this country, in the absence of drastic concomitant measures for limiting our exports to our imports. So long as it is possible for the "City" to expropriate our annual national industrial production, by issuing less domestic purchasing-power than will buy it all, and to export the "surplus" in exchange for Bonds for themselves and fodder for the nation at large, so long will the debtor-nations be compelled to undersell our own farmers as the only possible means of paying even the interest on their debts.   II 1

An increasing number of both public bodies and private individuals are beginning to ask the question: What is the

Government's policy in the matter of Agriculture? One of the world's practical experts in Food-production declared recently that we are in the midst of "the greatest struggle of modern times", the struggle between "Industry (so-called) and Agriculture"; and he added that "the country had got to make up its mind whether or not it was going forward on a basis of agricultural industry, and not on the basis of commercial industry any longer." Similarly, but in even more anguished terms, the Federation of British Industries [excluding the greatest of them all—Agriculture!] petitioned the Government to come to some decision, since, in the absence of a defined and long-range policy in regard to domestic Agriculture, it is impossible for other industrialists to plan ahead save in periods of months if not of weeks. It is easy enough to realize the difficulties in which the Government finds itself. Tossed between the conflicting "lobbies" of the representatives of both International and National financial interests, they are driven to pursue a course which in the end satisfies nobody and sacrifices everybody but the banks. On Mondays and Tuesdays the Government is protectionist and in favour of the widest possible extension of domestic food-production. On Wednesdays and Thursdays, the Dominions, Argentina, Denmark and all the rest are admitted under conditions at least approximating to Free Trade. And on Fridays and Saturdays somebody is allowed to prescribe Restriction of both Product and Output and simultaneously to destroy both fields and crops in the interests of an imaginary price-level. There is no wonder that with all these gyrations the heads of everybody concerned become dizzy, and nobody knows his right hand from his left. The decision that must ultimately be made is already written in the book of fate. As surely as primary nations are now rapidly becoming secondary also (adding

Industry to Agriculture) so surely must secondary countries become primary also (adding Agriculture to Industry). The period of transition may be longer or shorter, but it is already in process; and it is safe to say that within a generation the United Kingdom will be practically self-supporting as regards the products of Agriculture. A Government with a mind of its own would say this at once, whereupon long-range policies could be easily adapted to it.   V II

Everybody is now agreed that the plight of farming is desperate in the extreme and that nothing short of a *revolutionary* change of our monetary system can be of any use to it. The mere provision of cheap credits, even if under the existing bankers' rules it were possible, would be useless; and even a moratorium on the farmers' present interest-payments would scarcely delay their ruin by a week. Some are of the opinion that it is all a matter of prices. The prices now commanded in the open world market by our farmers are insufficient to cover their costs, let alone to leave any profit. Prices, they think, must therefore be raised. But to raise prices effectively must involve such an indirect taxation of the rest of the nation that, in effect, the final outcome would be not the relief of a grievance so much as its transfer to other shoulders. The truth of the matter is that the proposal to raise prices as presumably the means of enabling the farmers to recover their costs is suicidal. For by raising the prices of agricultural products the purchasing-power of the nation at large is correspondingly curtailed in other directions, with the final result that Peter the shoemaker is deprived of trade to provide Paul the farmer with a little more of it. The whole problem, it will appear, though indeed one of prices, is a problem not of raising prices but of considerably lowering them.

Never does it occur to our statesmen that since Prices express the relation between Goods and Money, consideration must be given to Money as well as to Goods. In terms of a rational economic system, it would seem to be the simplest thing in the world to equate the money factor with the factor of Production and to regulate the quantity and purchasing-power of Money (that is to say, Prices), not by reference to the occult principles of "Sound Finance", but by reference to the actual facts of total Production and total Consumption.

II 5

What is it exactly that the International Wheat Conference of 1933 agreed upon? First of all, to reduce the amount of wheat grown by the four chief wheat-exporting nations, secondly, to encourage the consumption of wheat everywhere; and thirdly, to discourage the increase of the wheat acreage in any of the now importing countries—our own, for example. Is there, we ask, any principle here embodied that is not as base as it is old, or whose adoption at the present juncture in world economic affairs is not a triumph for treachery and a model for an asylum? If it were the case that enough wheat is grown to ensure everybody in the world against starving for bread, it might be time to call a halt to the expenditure of further time and labour on its production. If the increased consumption of bread were proposed to be brought about by the only truly economic means of making it obtainable by everybody that needed it, the second article of the agreement might be commended. And, finally, if the home production of wheat were merely a matter of this or that luxury-article, the consent of our representatives to its future restriction might pass as a necessary concession to the demands of International Finance. But in the actual and known circumstances, that millions on the earth starve for want of bread, that the consumption of wheat is limited by its price, and that it is the obligation in every sense of every nation to grow as much of its own food as it possibly can, it is, as we say, nothing less than treacherous imbecility to arrive at this agreement and to demand that it shall be enforced.

Given a sufficient effective demand, in the form of purchasing-power or money distributed as a National Dividend or as a credit-subsidy to prices; given, further, what is already the fact, a progressive limitation of agricultural imports—it will be seen that we then have some of the conditions under which Agriculture was carried on during the war. If in those conditions, and with the handicap of insufficient and inefficient labour, this country nevertheless nearly succeeded in completely supporting itself, agriculturally speaking—it can confidently be predicted that in the same conditions with added advantages, and without any collectivization save that of credit, the nation could become completely self-supporting agriculturally with incalculable profit to itself in health as well as in wealth.   I 6

We are not saying that, in our judgment, it is necessarily desirable that this country should become self-sufficient in regard to Foodstuffs, even though it is undoubtedly true that as agricultural nations tend to become more and more industrialized, the former industrialized nations must become more and more agricultural, thus bringing about in each a balance of Production tending to self-sufficiency in respect of all staple commodities. All we are saying is that the unanimous assertion of the Press and the parrot in the street that this country *cannot* become self-sufficient in respect of Foodstuffs is not only false but knowably false to everybody who is prepared to pay Truth the compliment of recognition.

Apart from the practical assurance that any smallholder may acquire (we are speaking of Producing by permission of Nature, be it remembered, not of Selling by permission of the Banks); apart from a score of such assurances as the claim of the Fens, for example, to be able to produce the Nation's potatoes; there is the evidence of every competent practical expert that in fact it would be easy and not even difficult for this country so to increase its Food Production at home that the nation could be entirely self-sufficient. V 8

Why does the belief persist that we cannot grow our own foodstuffs? The answer may be stated in three points. One: since our Money-monopolists will not issue enough money at home to purchase the domestic production, the surplus has to be exported in the form of a foreign loan. Second: since the interest charges on foreign loans must be paid in Goods, the nation is bound to admit foreign Goods, chiefly agricultural, to the amount of the charge. Third: in order to persuade the country to accept such competitive imports, the financial authorities have to spread and maintain two lies—the lie that foreign food is cheaper than home-grown food, and the lie that we cannot possibly grow our own food-supplies. These delusions being firmly established in all minds save those occasionally awake, the rest is easy: the "City" can continue foreign lending, our farmers can be reduced to bank-slaves like their foreign rivals, home-grown foodstuffs can be destroyed, land put out of cultivation and crops restricted, while everybody still believes we cannot feed ourselves, and the whole nation continues to stagger to its doom. V 25

Industry

Since the purchasing-power distributed for actual

Consumption through the channels of Wages and Salaries necessarily diminishes, under the existing system, at the same rate at which machine-production increases, then, unless by some device, such as National Dividends or Price-reduction, the deficiency of distributed Purchasing is deliberately made up, the population must grow poorer and poorer as the productive resources of the nation grow greater and greater.   II 5

It might be supposed that at least during periods of depression, resulting from deflation, the growth of the world's productive plant would slow down. Extraordinarily enough, mechanical development seems to thrive equally well on deflation and inflation. When times are "prosperous", it is intelligible that new plant of all kinds should be laid down in abundance; but equally, it seems, when times are "depressed", new plant is, if not laid down in such abundance, intensified by inventive economy in terms of productivity.
                                                                                        I 22

In terms of calories the potential production of the United States to-day is 150,000 per head per annum against the beggarly 2000 of the ancient Empires. But will these facts outweigh the accumulated traditions of 7000 years of suffering under the curse laid upon Adam? Can the children of the yoke accept the Gospel of Man's redemption as promulgated through Watt's tea-kettle?   I 22

On the sick-bed, if not the death-bed, of Industrialism Mr. Henry Ford still affirms his inextinguishable faith in the future of Machinery. The industrial age, he says, has scarcely dawned as yet; we see only its first crude beginnings. Thanks to Machinery, aided more and more by Chemistry, Man can confidently look forward to a time when practically the whole of the work of necessary production can be done in a few hours of light labour, leaving Man free to develop himself at leisure in a secure and humane society. We have no doubt that Mr. Henry Ford has seen the vision; and, what is more, he has named the means. "Give the world", he says, "a money system that makes it easy for goods to flow from man to man, and all the present factories on earth could not begin to supply a tenth of the demand." Mr. Ford may not be as familiar with the mechanism of Money as with the mechanism of a car. But at least he is aware that the secret of the control of Industry lies in Money.   I 9

The fundamental error in our financial accountancy to which the deepening tragedy of the world is due can perhaps be illustrated by reference to the Coal Industry itself. It will not be denied that a great deal of bank-credit (that is, Bank-manufactured money) has been put into the organization and equipment of our coal-mines. Nor will it be denied that on the books of the mining concerns these credits rank as costs to be charged into the ultimate price paid by the consumer for coal. Other things, therefore, being equal, the greater the amount of bank-credit issued to or, as is said, invested in any industry, the higher the price necessarily charged to the ultimate consumer since the ultimate consumer is bound to pay not only for the (say) coal he consumes but, in addition, for both the repayment of the credits issued and for the depreciation of the total capital equipment. Even this mulcting of the consumer for the maintenance of the total capital equipment, whether in use or not, is not the whole story. For it has to be realized that even the initial issue of bank-credit has the precise effect of taxation, being as it is, inflation in the strict sense, namely, an increase of

Money unaccompanied by an immediate increase in Goods. The consumer, therefore, is stripped of purchasing-power both at the beginning and at the end of every industrial "enterprise". The issue of the credit to start it is an act of inflation which dilutes his immediate purchasing-power; and when, having thus virtually provided the capital with which coal can be produced, he is called upon, when consuming the coal, to repay his own credit to the issuing banks and also the charge of its total depreciation, he is stripped again. There need be little wonder that under this crazy system of book-keeping the world grows poorer at exactly the same rate that it grows richer; or that, in the case of Coal, for example, its retail price rises with the diminution of demand. Since all the "overheads" of the whole productive mechanism are charged to the retail prices of the goods actually offered for sale—there being, under the monopoly of Credit by the Banks, no other source from which they *can* be paid—it follows that as Industry develops and its capital equipment increases, retail prices *must* rise. Eventually the gap between the Means to Produce and the Means to Buy becomes so great that nobody can buy what everybody has to sell.   I 12

Lancashire is not famous outside the country for intelligence; but there is one thing the Banker will find it hard to make Lancashire mill-owners swallow, and that is the necessity to break up their beautiful machinery. The appeal of the representatives of the debenture holders—namely, the Banks—to the cotton-factory owners (if they can be so dignified) to "rationalize" their industry by scrapping plant was met with a thoroughly irrational but reasonable refusal. Why, in any sacred name, should machinery be scrapped while the need for its product, as testified by a shirtless world, is still beyond the capacity of existing machinery? The difficulty is still further complicated by the perfectly human factor presented by the choice of the victims: who is to be the first? And, finally, there is in Lancashire the ineradicable optimism of the English expressing itself in the simple faith that things will pick up if only they hang on. Unfortunately, however, there are occasions when not to know that you are beaten is a crime, and this is one of them. Beyond all the great industries of this country, Cotton has lost its premier exporting future for ever. Coal may come back again by the discovery of some new use for our relative monopoly. The steel trade, if America goes out of world-business, may revive for a time. But cotton, having no natural monopoly of material, skill, machinery, or, in these days, of climate, its value in terms of export is little more than the bargain counter within measurable years.   I 11

Industrial Dictatorship

With the best will in the world to provide ideal conditions for the workers of all kinds actually engaged in the Production of economic Goods and Services (incidentally, the higher services to society are seldom economic), it cannot be claimed that their output, the total annual Production, is even preponderantly their own. Not only is it true, as Christianity asserts, that every living member of the community contributes in one form or another to the total wealth of the community, but 95 per cent of the actual output arising from the actual labour of the actual workers is the fruit of the accumulated machinery, skill, organization and social history of past generations. Without intending to belittle the services rendered to Industry by the "workers" or to compare them to their disadvantage with the services rendered by the other indispensable factors in society, it is nevertheless only fair to remind them that, in point of fact, the vast majority of them are only machine-minders. We are all, indeed, in the strictest sense, tenants only of the national inheritance; and since, as co-heirs, we have each of us a just claim on the national patrimony, there can be no question, in right, of the dictatorship of its mere administrators. To those who dispute the communal right of Consumption, there is, however, only one effective reply in the long run, it is that their theories will not work. And they will work less and less as the factor of human labour diminishes in importance relatively to the increasing factor of social inheritance.   III 26

The whole theory of the sovereign right of the Producer to anything more than the *administration* of Production is totally false and, consequently, in practice, totally ruinous both to the Producer himself and to the community at large. This is not to say that the Producer of Goods and Services is not entitled to all and more than all of the favourable conditions specified—ample payment, the best of working conditions, the minimum of labour and the maximum of leisure. But to pass from the provision of these favourable conditions for the fulfilment of a communal function to the admission of the right of the Producer to dictate communal policy is simply to propose to set up one dictatorship for another. That Production is indispensable to the very exist-ence of a community is a truism. But it is no less obvious that Defence, Science, and a score of other directly unpro-ductive services are equally indispensable to the life and well-being of a community. And if it be right that the Producer should dictate policy on the ground that his function is in-dispensable, a similar right and for the same reason must be accorded to all the rest.   III 26

I

It is "contrary to all the public interest" embodied in the conception of a free democratic society to permit any body of men, however qualified, to exercise dictatorship of no matter what kind. As an alternative to the dictatorship now exercised (invisibly to most) by the Monopolists of the Financial system, the dictatorship exercised by a group of engineers is perhaps to be preferred, but only, we believe, as the frying-pan to the fire. For inevitably, as in the case of all dictatorships, the special interests of the group would prevail over their social interests; and in place of our present all-powerful oligarchy mad about Money-power, society would find itself ridden by an oligarchy mad about mechanical Energy.   II 13

National Planning

There is not the least doubt that if Planning be adopted the consequences to the "consumer", not privileged by pull to buy Torgsin, will be that, in putting the Producers in control, the Consumer is bound to be subordinated. But is it in the least degree desirable that the Producer should be placed in control? Even on the reasonable supposition that certain planning of Production will be necessary even in the best ordered Social Credit state, is that Planning to be adopted *before* the community as consumer has recovered its rights over its own spending-power; and to be at the whim and discretion of the operators of the social productive mechanism? If a planned society is instituted, its organizers will insist upon determining not only the plans, but the objective of the plans. The community, in short—the sovereign by right of eminent domain—by empowering certain of its agents to "plan" Production, will in fact be putting the whole economic life of the nation into the hands of a small group of technical "experts". But between allowing the Producers complete control of their technique, and allowing them to control the distribution of the product (99 per cent of which, in any case, is due to the social factor in all production), there is all the difference between making the cook the master of the kitchen and permitting him to become the tyrant of the household. If the choice, in fact, is between Production and Distribution controlled, as now, by the Financial Monopoly (the system miscalled Capitalism by the victims of Marx) and Production and Distribution controlled by State Corporations under the plea of "Planning", we are all for the Financial Monopoly. Fortunately, however, the choice is not between King Log and King Stork except for frogs. The actual choice is between Planning before or Planning after the restoration of the community's control over both its Production and its Consumption.   V 23

UNEMPLOYMENT

It is impossible to pronounce a civilization dead until it has been dead for many years. Rome took a long time to complete its fall. But it is the truth, bitter in one sense, healing in another, that so long as Unemployment continues to be regarded as a diseased condition to be "cured" and not as a symptom of health to be accepted and encouraged, so long is our industrial civilization on its way to death.   II 24

The fact is, of course, that Unemployment is a machine product, the output of which increases with the use of machinery, and not even universal slave labour could absorb the inevitably growing volume of the unemployed.   I 26

Work and Wages
        The modern world is still in doubt, and will probably remain in painful indecision for a few years longer, suspended, like Mahomet's coffin, between Heaven and Hell. Without pretending that Unemployment has never existed in the world before—we recall the Bread and Circuses of ancient Rome—it is nevertheless safe to say that Unemployment has never existed before on the present scale, on a mathematically increasing scale, and side by side with, and as a direct consequence of, an increasing Productivity due to the use of mechanical power. It follows that the decision to be made by mankind today is both momentous and unique in the history of the world, and hence that the best minds must not dare to be indifferent to it—will not

be, and cannot be, in fact. The alternatives, moreover, chance to be singularly clear and singularly concrete; they are not of the order of metaphysics. On the one hand, and merely as a practical possibility actualizable within a measurable period of only months, we have the prospect of an Age of Plenty for All, and, moreover, without violent revolution, or confiscation, or Fascism, or Communism, or class strife, or even that "levelling" of incomes so beloved of the envious. The concrete means, in the form of raw materials, mechanical equipment, skill and organization, are most undoubtedly there; and they are indefinitely expansible. At the same time, the legislative means are there, in the form of the proposed National Credit Account, the institution of the compensated Price, and National Dividends. That is the "solution" offered by Social Credit both to the so-called problem of Unemployment and to the vaster and more real problem of the future of Mankind in relation to Machinery. On the other hand, we have the prospect—equally if not more realizable—opened up to us, not by Science, but by the mere inertia of the forces now moving according to habit and vested interests. The prejudices to be encountered before the Age of Plenty can be actually willed into being may be reduced to these: the conviction that Work, in the sense of paid labour, is not only good in itself but indispensable both to Production and to Morality; that Industry must therefore be maintained, not only as the best means of getting the best things done in the best possible way, but as an agency for providing employment and cheating Satan—that is to say, as a moral agency of government; and, consequently, that "Unemployment" must always be looked upon as a regrettable maladjustment to be "cured" as quickly as possible.

Supplementing these prejudices and both pandering to

them and fostering them are, of course, the "vested interests" of Money and the rest of the "authorities". But it is of more importance at this moment to consider what is likely to be the outcome of the combined prejudices and interests that are now in control of the nation's future, and especially as they are likely to operate through the "problem" of Unemployment.

(1) Premising, as we have seen, that "Employment" is healthy, and "Unemployment" vicious when voluntary, and a social disease when not, the combined authorities will move hell and earth to provide Employment by every means in their power, short of the complete sabotage of Science. Since there are only two ways of providing full Employment—namely, by the Export of Credit and by Public Works—increasing foreign competition may be looked for, together with an increasing tendency to adopt the policy of Public Works as foreign investment ceases to be possible. The former of these two devices will lead to war; and the latter to an increasing burden of debt and taxation.

(2) To stave off as long as possible both War and the revolt of the taxpayer, the authorities will devise measures of increasing ingenuity for parking the Unemployed on the incomes of the Employed *by indirect means*. Unemployment Insurance, for instance, involves a tax on the individual additional to the tax imposed by the State. Voluntary donations to the Unemployed, again, are a form of taxation none the less real, and often onerous, for being only morally exacted.

(3) Still from the point of view that "Employment" is normal and "Unemployment" demoralizing, increasing efforts will be made to keep the Unemployed "fit" for Employment. Not Bread and Circuses for the workless, but Bread and Camps.

(4) In spite of all these measures, and because of some of them, not only, however, will the ratio of the Unemployed to the Employed continue to increase; but, before very long, still more drastic means of "training" the Unemployed will be resorted to. In the end these measures will lead either to social revolt or to the re-institution of practically unveiled slavery, and to the end of any hope for human civilization that is not merely class culture.

These two pictures may appear to be fanciful, the latter no less than the former. But no student of history capable of reading contemporary events historically can have any doubt that at any rate the latter prospect is already in course of rapid realization.   IV 5

It is a characteristic of an over-trained mentality that not only does a simple problem appear to it as vastly complicated, but the solutions it offers are as a rule so wildly irrelevant. Why, in the first place, is the problem of the distribution of an existing and potential Plenty (which a good Army Commissariat could arrange) invariably and gratuitously paraphrased by such minds as the complex and, in fact, insoluble, problem of providing *work* for everybody? Is it inconceivable to the medieval schoolmen that an income of demand-tokens representing a dividend on the national wealth may be both more easily and more economically allotted to individuals for the maintenance of their leisure than in return for their enforced participation in what is called work? Apart from the fact that, if civilization and science continue, it is inevitable that the total possible amount of work will prove increasingly insufficient to go round, so that eventually if not immediately it will be necessary to provide incomes otherwise than through the agency of "employment", what is the prospect here and now of distributing the existing Plenty if the only means to be allowed are "employment"? II 23

Work and Morality

There are, it may be, fossilized intelligences still capable of believing that "work", in the sense of involuntary toil for wages, is the onlie begetter of real enjoyment of the fruits of Man's conquest of Nature. Before he was booted out of Paradise, Adam to these was a miserable shirker suffering from shame for his parasitic idleness, while afterwards he became ennobled by the sweat of his brow. On the other hand, even among the most obscurantist of moralists there can be no individual with any pretensions to a mind who can persuade himself for an instant that the two million-odd of our Unemployed—to say nothing of the Unemployed in America and elsewhere—are ever again going to be in a position to enjoy the "best income" if it means working for wages for it. IV 7

Among the consequences of the belief that Employment is a good in itself and Unemployment an evil is the belief that any work that yields employment is laudable: the end justifies the means. Only this explanation can conceivably excuse what otherwise must be regarded as a lapse into barbarism on the part of several Members of Parliament that Huns would envy. Gratuitously interrupting questions in the House of Commons on the supply of bombing aeroplane engines to Germany, a Unionist member protested that the orders meant "a considerable increase in the volume of employment", and, as such, were to be welcomed instead of criticized. The same sub-human morality, of course, is responsible for the supply of arms to the Bolivian and Paraguyan natives foully murdering each other for the privilege of becoming victims of the successful bondholders; and that it should pass in the House of Commons without protest is evidence of the submergence of humanity under the stress of the superstition of Work. We have, we fear, still to experience depths beyond depths of atrocity in the pursuit of this "cure" for Unemployment. Exactly as savages are driven to cannibalism in the belief that human flesh is indispensable to their healthy existence, our contemporary business men, tutored by the witch-doctors of Finance, are persuaded that anthropophagy is no crime when it provides the tribe with the magic elixir called Work. And exactly as, in the end, the dearer the victim the greater the virtue inhaled by his savage murderers, so, as time goes on, the supply of armaments to the nation's enemies even in war-time will become a justifiable means of Employment in the eyes of the ministrants of our contemporary Black Mass.   V 6

Unemployment a Sign of Social Health

Everybody outside the Government at Whitehall and Threadneedle Street is now aware that Unemployment is irremediable for the simple reason that it is not a disease but a symptom of health; and everybody not paid to think otherwise is aware that the proper treatment of Unemployment is to regard it as socially earned leisure and to provide for it, not out of the pockets of the active participants in Production, but out of the National Credit. With serene indifference, however, to enlightened opinion everywhere, the "authorities", that is to say, the monopolists of the Money-system, continue in their course as if public opinion were nothing to them. Public opinion, indeed, was dismissed as dogs that bark while the caravan passes on. So long as the caravan can continue to pass on, and all that public opinion will do is to bark at it, so long, it is certain, will the Money-Monopolists feel secure.   III 26

What is the sense in maintaining that Employment is the ideal when, in fact, its general realization is increasingly impossible except at the cost of the retrogression of society from Science to Barbarism? Not only, we repeat with the patience of a recurring decimal, is Unemployment not a disease, but, whether a disease or not, it is incurable. There may be, we do not deny, moments of apparent recovery due to injections of public works, foreign orders on credit, or occasional gaps in the actual foreign market; just as in the trench-warfare of the late lamented War salients were occasionally taken; but exactly as it is now agreed that only the exhaustion of human nature would have ended the trench-war in the absence of the providential intervention of a novel factor, it can be confidently said that, short of a saving "brainwave", there is no possible end to Unemployment.   IV 5

So long as the creation of the means of Leisure which we owe to Science is regarded as a symptom of disease and subjected to prescriptions of cure, so long, we may be certain, will all the proposed "remedies" prove to be either impractical or useless. There literally is no cure for Unemployment that is compatible with the continued existence and development of applied Science. The Soviet Government claims that it alone has solved the great problem of modern society by setting and keeping all its people at work. But apart from the undesirability of the means, the special circumstances of a backward people westernizing themselves in a short spasm, and the absurdity of subordinating the proper objective of Industry, namely, the production and distribution of the best goods in the best way, to the moral objective of providing as much work as possible for as many as possible, it is also completely certain that in proportion as the various Plans succeed, Unemployment will begin to be created in Russia exactly as it has been created in the countries that have had a longer industrial development.

By taking it for granted, that Unemployment must be treated as a disease to be cured, the House of Commons, all unwittingly we hope, played perfectly, as they have so many times before, into the hands of the Financial villains of the social peace. So long as Parliament and even the Labour members can be persuaded that Unemployment is a temporary regrettable phenomenon which the Government is trying to deal with, if only the rest of the world will let it, so long will they keep their eyes and ears closed to the real facts. It is no wonder, now we come to think of it, that the message of Technocracy was immediately drowned by the bellowing of the fatted Beaverbrooks. The message of Technocracy was that not only is Unemployment (defined as the substitution of natural for human energy) an inevitable concomitant of Progress, but its rate of increase is directly proportional to the pace of technological development. To the Financial dictators and their moral agents, the prospect of a society in which the sanction of starvation is no longer in their possession must be nothing less than terrifying. How would they get their morning coffee if they could not starve a man for failing to bring it?

Unemployment, we repeat, is so far from being a disease that it has been and is the deliberate aim of intelligence since Man was expelled from Paradise. Labour-saving devices have paved the road of human progress; and it is nothing less than black ingratitude to human reason to consider as a social disease what, in fact, is a social triumph.   III 17

Employment v. Science

Truly enough, the provision of work for all is perfectly possible. Give us a free hand and no conscience and we will undertake to have the whole population engaged in work and getting paid for it. All we have to do is to invent a planet with an unlimited demand for our manufactures and after dumping the supplies in the Arctic Seas, to return with paper acknowledgments of debt which the banks would discount. In less than a couple of months England would be buzzing with industry like a hive of insane bees. Short of some such piece of lunacy, however, there is literally no possibility of providing work for all or for more than a progressively diminishing proportion of people. Science is at war with Employment and its victories are Unemployment. And since not even the most reactionary of dictators has as yet forbidden the march of Science and Invention, the odds on Science against Unemployment are as Geometric to Arithmetic Progression.   V 5

The effect of insisting that work alone shall be the prior condition of the receipt of purchasing-power is naturally that everybody who cannot beg or steal attempts to find or to create a "job" for himself in industry that shall qualify him to live. And the effect of this, again, is to ruin Industry from the standpoint of efficiency by exposing it to the incursions of hordes of citizens looking to it for the provision of the right to live.   III 8

The worst thing to be said of these semi-compulsory schemes for providing work for the Unemployed is that they point to servility exactly when the facts point to increased freedom. As fast, indeed, as the creative genius of

Man liberates men from slavery to the machine, the evil genius of Man claps them into prison again.   III 1

The Dole

It is very little use, at this late date, to attempt to defend the "Dole", invaluable as it has been and may continue to be as an insurance against the spread of Communism in this country. On reflection, however, if anybody is now capable of it, it will be realized that the unpopularity of the Dole, among the classes who object to it, is due to its defects rather than to its positive qualities. In the first place, the "Dole" is paid at the expense of other individuals, that is to say, by direct or indirect subtraction from existing purchasing-power. In the second place, unlike pensions, retiring allowances and other forms of "money for nothing", it is small enough to be socially contemptible. And, in the third place, it is confined to a more or less accidental category of citizens and awarded as a charity rather than as a matter of right and justice. But these defects are, it is obvious—but again only upon reflection—easily remediable. There is not the least reason why the "Dole", or, for the matter of that, any other social service, should be paid for out of the *incomes* of the people at large or any class of it. There exists a source, relatively inexhaustible and constantly increasing, which competent economists define as the Real Credit of the nation (in other words, its ability to produce and deliver Goods and Services) upon which not only do all our present consumers draw, but upon which the community in its collective capacity could draw without prejudice to any present consumer. The nation has only to establish a National Real Credit Account showing the true state of affairs in terms of Potential Production, and then to translate the same into a National Financial Credit Account, to find itself in possession of a fund as unlimited in terms of Money as the nation is in real Production. Payment for the social services now accounted into the Budget and charged to the rate- and taxpayers should and would thereafter be made from the National Credit Account. The amount, again, of the existing "Dole" could be increased until it became respectable to take it; and, finally, the present discrimination of its recipients could be abolished by the simple device of making it universal. History will show, we believe, and within a few years, that the despised "Dole" was the precursor of the National Dividend; and that once more the world will have been saved by a birth in a manger.   II 1

Mr. Baldwin once discovered and drew attention to a "curious phenomenon", namely, that while there had been a rise in the unemployment figures, there had been no corresponding decrease in the volume of industrial production. And he drew from it, astonishingly enough, the right conclusion, namely, that we are producing more with fewer men. There is, of course, nothing "curious", in the sense of novel, in the phenomenon whatever, since the whole aim of mechanical invention is to produce more and more with less and less human labour. The curiosity of the phenomenon is that Mr. Baldwin and the world in general remain unaware both of the fact and of its implications. Mechanical invention, it may be said, is the first effective challenge that Man has made to the curse laid upon Adam that only in the sweat of his brow should he eat bread. By calling upon and harnessing to his own needs the higher powers of the solar energies Man has succeeded in so completely escaping the curse that an almost paradisaical state of leisure for everybody is well within his reach. What is it that still forbids the once exiled and cursed Adam to return in conscious triumph of conquest to the state from which he once fell? The answer is another Adam, Adam Smith, who, formulating the "laws" of economics *before the machine was invented* (he was a contemporary of Watt), managed to impose upon subsequent generations down to the present the principles of a past age of scarcity. It is improbable that had Adam Smith lived to see the storm that has arisen in Watt's tea-kettle he would not have realized the need to reformulate his economic generalizations. Unlike his successors he was not case-hardened in his own traditions. And it is probable that he would have realized that unless for each additional unit of mechanical productivity society deliberately created a new unit of purchasing power, the gulf between Production and Consumption would continue to widen at precisely the same rate as the progress of mechanical invention. A critical phase has now been reached in this process that began with Watt, and Mankind has now a decision to make of the greatest significance for its future. Is Machinery to be destroyed and the world re-submitted to the curse of the first Adam? Or, in defiance of both Adams, is Man to use Machinery for the very purpose for which he invented it—to save labour and create leisure? That, in simple terms, is the world-theme of our age; and it seems impossible to defer decision, passively or actively, any longer.   I 12

TAXATION AND NATIONAL BUDGETS

The Principles

There has nowhere been any radical discussion of the Budget or of the principles of our taxation. The consequence is that though everybody complains, and very justly, nobody can dispute what the Chancellor of the Exchequer calls the "simple arithmetic" of his preposterous case. The Budget and Government finance, however, rest in general on certain false presuppositions which, like Topsy, have simply growed, until they have now become the unquestioned postulates of every Chancellor and, for the matter of that, of every victimized taxpayer. The first postulate is that the costs of Government must be charged, not to the national production, taken as a whole, of the budgetary year, but to the earnings of the other parties, individuals and corporations. And the second postulate is like unto the first, namely, that apart from the individual incomes of the Government's fellow-contributories to the national annual production, there exists no source from which the Government services to the nation can be paid. From these suppositions, both totally false, there inevitably follow the results with which we are only too familiar: lamentations on the part of the individual taxpayer at the ever-growing cost of Government services and pitiful cries for more and more economy "axes"; and, on the other side, frantic searches for "fresh sources of revenue" with constant anxiety lest the limit of the endurance of the taxpayers should be reached.

Now of what does the National Wealth consist? Beyond any possibility of even "expert" doubt, the National Wealth consists of two kinds of goods: Goods actual and Goods potential, Goods ready for use and Goods in the form of the means to make them. In a simple phrase, our National Wealth is composed of the things we already have and our means to make more of them. Of these two kinds of goods, the Actual and the Potential, which together constitute our National Wealth, which is the greater in value and amount? Perfectly correct! The Goods actual form at any given moment a mere fraction of the Goods potential, just as the actual apple-crop of a season is a mere fraction of the apple-potential of the enduring orchard. It is, moreover, a constantly diminishing fraction. Thanks to Science, Invention and Engineers, the difference in amount between the Actual and the Potential of the National Wealth is constantly increasing in favour of the Potential. And this is true even during periods when the production of Goods actual appears to be at the maximum of capacity. During the War, for example, the production of Goods actual was stupendous. Never in the history of man were such quantities of Goods actual produced before. Actual Production was so gigantic that even its wholesale destruction by millions of experts entirely failed to keep up with it; and we finished the war with a surplus of Goods actual which would have kept the nation in luxury for at least a year. Not even the most thorough-going Individualist will deny that the State, through its official agents, renders service and contributes to the total national production; and not even the most Muscovite of Communists will deny the contribution made by the private individual. The question at issue, in respect of the principles of the Budget and Taxation in general, is not whether these two factors do or

K

should contribute relatively more or relatively less to the
common total, but whether each is fully entitled to be paid
out of the joint and common product. If the answer is Yes,
as it must be, then all there is to be said is that our present
system of Taxation stands condemned in principle. For far
from being paid directly, or indirectly, out of the common
product we call the National Wealth, the services rendered
to this product by the agencies called the State are paid for
out of the pockets of those other contributory agencies
described as taxpayers. The situation is precisely similar to
one in which a father is engaged on a job with his sons and
takes his wage out of their pockets, instead of out of the
job itself. Thanks to this naïve practice of not charging
State-services to the common product, namely, the National
Wealth, but to the earnings of the other services, we have
the spectacle in every nation of State and Individuals at
cross-purposes, with the State in the role of robber and
the individual in the role of the victim.

The simple fact about Money is that there is literally not
enough of it. With a trifling exception, there is only just
enough money in existence as a rule to represent and command that fraction, that diminishing fraction, of the National
Wealth which consists of Goods actual. There is practically
no money in existence to correspond with or to give any
individual a call upon that major constituent of the national
product which consists of Goods potential. The result is that
unless the State can pick the pockets of the monetary wage-
earners, it has, under our existing system, nowhere else
to turn for money. The remedy for this state of affairs, when
the anomaly has been clearly seen, is simple enough. It is
to make, issue and distribute money at the same rate at
which Goods of both kinds are made, so that at any given
moment the correspondence between the power of Demand

represented by money-tickets in possession of the nation, and the power of Supply represented by the National Wealth as a whole, is that of an accountant's balance.

We cannot see reality for money and our "experts" least of all. But here let us add that a part of the blindness at least is deliberate and that still more of it is induced by an interested if instinctive propaganda. Money is, in one sense, a commodity like any other. It happens, however, to be the one commodity whose employment as a "carrier" is indispensable in every exchange of commodities that is not simple barter. The demand for it is therefore universal, and grows with the multiplication of goods and the occasions of their exchange. We are attributing no particular viciousness to the people who happen, by accident or ability, to find themselves in possession and control of this unique commodity, if we take it for granted that their attitude towards Money is the attitude of most other Monopolists to the object of their monopoly. That is to say, their attitude is one of self-preservation coupled with a lively anxiety for the maintenance of their paramount privilege. The monopolists of Money, furthermore, differ in no respect from other unqualified Monopolists in their choice of means both of exercising and preserving their monopoly. They maintain its price by restricting its supply and are hostile to any criticism, and still more to any proposal to limit their absolute authority. The means they have invented for themselves of restricting the supply of Money, and thus of keeping the price high, are known to everybody as the Gold Standard —a device so patent, since the same Monetary Monopolists are also the virtual monopolists of Gold, that it is nothing short of amazing that it has escaped the detection even of "experts". By monopolizing the manufacture of the unique commodity of Money, by arbitrarily limiting its supply

to a multiple of Gold, and by persuading everybody that
the science of Money is known only to "experts", the
Money-monopolists or bankers contrive not only to drive
a rack-renting bargain with the community in respect of
every single economic transaction, but, a thousand times
worse, they make it impossible for the community, consisting of the State and its citizens, to draw upon any part
of the National Wealth except by their permission. The
point cannot be too clearly realized, since obviously the
future of society depends upon it. By restricting the amount
of Money in circulation (for their own profit and power)
to a fraction only of the National Wealth, the banks, we
say, virtually compel the State either to rob its citizens of
their hard-earned money by infamous taxation or to go
cuffs on wrists to the bankers for what in their jargon is
called "accommodation", that is to say, for "new" or
additional money. And even for this they must pledge a
portion of the Potential Production and pay interest upon
it.

Without dwelling longer upon the iniquities of the
Money Monopoly, we content ourselves for the present
with stating two relevant and irrefutable facts. In the first
place, so far from being obliged to cut down either our
National or our individual consumption by reason of any
shortage of Production or of the Means of Production
(other, of course, than those of Money), the National
Wealth of England is sufficient to meet an annual Government Budget of ten or twenty times the amount of the
present Budget, without drawing upon the Wages, Salaries
or Dividends of its citizens for a single penny. And, in the
second place, so far from there being any need (again, of
course, than a monetary need) for any curtailment of our
expenditure, national or individual, the crying need of an

expanding Production, the very condition of its continued expansion, is a correspondently expanding consumption, that is, in the monetary sense, of spending. The only difficulty in the way is not a physical or natural difficulty at all. The National Wealth is not imaginary even if most of it is only Potential. Its amount, moreover, can be and often has been sufficiently accurately estimated; and the physical means for its actualization and distribution truly exist. The only difficulty—and let nobody under-estimate it—is in the power of the Money monopoly to maintain itself by the usual means—employed, in this instance, with the highest degree of cunning—of restricting the access of the nation to its own wealth by monopolizing the golden key.   I 2

Accounting, Public and Private

The problem of Public Finance, simply stated, is to discover a means whereby the State can undertake public works of any socially desirable kind without ruining the community by murderous taxation; or alternatively, how to reduce its expenditure in relief of taxation without committing suicide as a State. It has been suggested that the public authority (e.g. the London County Council) should present its accounts in the form in which accounts are presented by any private Corporation and offset its current expenditure by the appreciation of its capital plant—by doing which, it is claimed, the public authority might frequently show a surplus rather than a deficit in its Balance-sheet. And following a somewhat similar form of reasoning the "New Republic" once proposed to balance the State budget by crediting the State with the full value of its capital expenditure during the accounting period. The suggestions, however, are in both cases, though in the right direction, altogether too timid and trifling. It is true that the secret flaw in the existing monetary system is, at bottom, a flaw in book-keeping, and hence that the remedy is to be found in a reformed accountancy, but it is useless to look for the flaw in our Public accounts by reference to the assumed model of private Corporation accounts, since there is anything but an exact parallel between them. Corporation accounts, it is obvious, presuppose a National monetary system; they take the Monetary system imposed on them for granted and trade in its tokens within the rules laid down. Public Accounts, on the other hand, and, in particular, the National Account annually rendered in the Budget, have an entirely different status, deriving, as they do, not from a Monetary system imposed by a higher authority but from a Monetary system created and subject to alteration by itself. It is therefore misleading to compare the accountancies of National and Corporate bodies as if, in fact, their status were similar. The Nation is in the last resort the creator of the very financial tokens with which Corporations trade.

II 20

Taxation and Social Credit

To the question at immediate issue, that of Taxation, the first of the three main principles of Social Credit are directly applicable. It is affirmed as a matter of equity and not of argument that the community in its historic continuity is the sole rightful owner of the whole of the communal wealth. In the community (at least intermediately) every Jack one of us, prince or pauper, banker or busman, lives and breathes and has his economic being. But this communal wealth, it is contended, that owes its creation, preservation and continuous appreciation to the community (admittedly through the agency of individuals) is at present instrumented by a Monetary system that, in the first place, is controlled by a private corporation, chartered, it is true, but a private monopoly still, and in the second place, that fails to reflect, and indeed, does not aim at reflecting, either the actual state of the communal wealth or, still less, the public policy implicit in the fact of community. Being concerned only with the legal tokens of real wealth, and trading directly only in these, the chartered Monopolists of our financial ticket system consciously or unconsciously aim always at enhancing the price of their commodity (Money) by keeping it in short supply, never giving but always lending it, charging the maximum interest for its use and selling it in the dearest market regardless of the interests of the community at large—with the consequence that neither the community in its corporate aspect as the State nor the individual citizen has right of access to or enjoyment of their common heritage and creation except upon terms dictated by the private interests of the monopolists of Money. Unable to realize that each of the two parties— State and Individual—is, in fact, restricted in access to their joint wealth by the restriction imposed on both by the private Money system, each is bound to regard the other as his natural enemy. To the State the Individual taxpayer is a disagreeable if pitiable creature constantly demanding more for less; and reciprocally to the Individual the State is a pitiless ogre constantly offering less for more. Reconciliation between these two complementary elements of the community is impossible in the presence of a Monetary monopoly. On the contrary, their conflict must intensify until one or the other is completely subordinated. It is, therefore, affirmed as the first principle of Social Credit that a Financial System must be made to reflect, and continuously to reflect, the facts of the communal real economic situation; and that to this end it is necessary to establish a

National Credit Account with, so to say, parallel columns for Real and Financial Capital, Expenditure (Consumption), Income (Production), Profit (Appreciation of Capital) and National Dividends (Profit-sharing). Upon such a National Credit Account both the State and the Individual would be able to draw as partners, and neither at the expense of the other. Taxation of the individual for revenue would be superfluous. At the same time the public services could be generously maintained. State and individual would be reconciled in Community.   II 21

The brighter our prospects of real Production become (thanks to the increasing success of our scientists in transferring work from human to mechanical agencies, thereby reducing the ratio of money-earnings to collective costs and prices), the blacker becomes the prospect of balancing the Budget by the taxation of individual incomes. Only when the present canons of sound finance are completely discredited and the National Financial Treasury becomes the book-keeper of the National Real Treasury—the nation's ability to Produce—will it be as possible as easy to balance both national and individual budgets simultaneously. II 22

We have not the smallest doubt that to the vast majority of people, accustomed naturally to thinking of economics in terms of their own personal budgets, the proposition that the nation, like the individual, must live within its income must appear self-evident. But the difference between an individual budget and a national budget is the difference between the transitory individuals, composing a whole, and the permanent whole itself. Collectively, it cannot be doubted, the nation is not only the sovereign proprietor and everlasting beneficiary of the total wealth of the historic community, but it is also the ultimate source of the money-tokens representing that wealth. And by virtue of the fact that the State permanently "owns" all the real wealth there is, both accumulated and current, and can instrument its use and distribution by means of its sovereign prerogative of creating money, whereas an individual owns only temporarily and can obtain money, not by "making" it, but only after it has been made, there can be, and there is, no parallel between the individual and the national budgets.

Again it cannot be said that in terms of Income the two parties are in any way comparable. Individual incomes are composed in terms of money, but the "income" of the collective nation cannot be said to consist of money at all —since money is the State's creation. The nation's real annual income, on the other hand, consists of the increment of its total wealth in terms of Production (Production minus Consumption), and not only, of course, in terms of actual output, but, as a major factor, in terms of potential production. To confuse this annual increment of total national real wealth, measurable in terms of ability to Produce, with the sum of the annual monetary payments made to the contributories to that increment, is to confuse real economics with financial economics. It must also be obvious that not only is the monetary income of the nation as individuals a very inadequate measure of the real increment of the nation's wealth (a new process, for example, costing in wages and salaries a few hundred pounds may increase the national real wealth by millions), but for the State, representing the nation, to tax the individual monetary incomes of its citizens when, in fact, the whole annual increment of real wealth is at its disposal (and the right of creating money to instrument it), is the collective gratuitous robbery of the individual. It is moreover demonstrable that the policy involved in reckoning as the annual income merely the monetary payments dispersed to individuals is bound sooner or later to end in disaster, for the reason that the sum of the monetary incomes of all the component individuals of the nation becomes less and less able to make an effective demand on the total national wealth. The result of it all must be exactly what we see today, that in proportion as the nation's real wealth measured in terms of potential Production increases, the purchasing-power of its citizens diminishes. And as the purchasing-power of its citizens diminishes, the annual "output" of goods in proportion to means of Production diminishes, with the final result that the State finds its sources of taxation drying up at the same rate at which its potential wealth increases.

Fragmentarily and inadequately as the idea is here indicated, we may hope, perhaps, that both the direction of the thought and its possible practical application to our national Budget are at least dimly visible. Let it be assumed, for instance, that the Chancellor of the National Exchequer, instead of reckoning the national income as the sum of the payments made to individuals in the form of Wages, Salaries, Profits and Dividends, reckons the national income in the financial equivalent of the net increase of the national Productivity. In the first place, since this annual increment in real wealth is considerably greater than can be drawn upon by the sum of the annual payments made to individuals, there is obviously no need for the State, as the administrator of the total national wealth, to take its expenses out of the pockets of its virtual employees. There is no need, that is to say, for taxation. And, in the second place, since it is not alone the annual increment or profit of the national wealth that is susceptible of distribution (whether among individuals or for State purposes) but the fruit of the whole corpus of the national Productive Wealth, there is not only possible, but there is urgently called for, simultaneously with the complete remission of taxation of the individual for revenue, the distribution to the individual of an annual dividend on the national patrimonial estate. Under these conditions, the position both of the Chancellor of the National Exchequer and of individual citizens would be enviable. The individual would obtain a purchasing-power consisting of a dividend on the "fruits of national association" (the accumulated common wealth of the community) in addition to his income from services currently rendered—his wages, salary and profits. And the National Chancellor equally would be able to draw upon the same national fund for the maintenance and improvement of the realm collectively. II 5

Assuming that the State, the source of Money, finances its expenditures, not fresh from its own resources, but from the monies previously issued and still circulating among its citizens, the effect can only be to diminish the spending-power of its citizens *pari passu* with the enlargement of the productive resources of the community collectively; that is to say, to widen still further the gulf between Productivity and Consumption. Whether or not it is possible, within the time allowed us, to transform our accountancy system in respect of private business—Capitalism at large—will depend, in our judgment, on the solution of the prior problem of public finance. Not Capitalism, in the sense defined, will be the first to break down; but the collapse of Capitalism will itself be preceded and, indeed, brought about, by the failure of the State to adapt its own financial mechanism to the requirements and facts of modern industry. Should it prove to be the case, as in all probability it will, that the next and ensuing Budgets will conceal a deficit not of a few millions, but of tens if not hundreds of millions, the situation, unless dealt with in a new way, and by a complete revolution in the conduct of Public as distinct from Private finance, will infallibly entail the destruction of the Capitalist system. But in that event, the Capitalist system will not have fallen by its own hand, but in consequence of the failure of statesmen to separate Public from Private finance. Its death and all its consequences will lie at the door of the Chancellor and the Treasury. I 15

Substitute for Taxation

State expenditure is of the nature of "overheads" on the total national economic system, and as the economic system as a whole becomes inevitably more and more a matter of the maintenance of national capital values, the expenditure on State services is bound to increase faster than the sum of the collective payments made to working individuals. The conclusion is obvious that if State expenditure is to be limited to the collective monetary income of its working citizens, either the latter will have to suffer a progressive taxation until they are crushed beneath its weight—in other words, until all incentive to work has disappeared—or, on the other hand, the State itself will be compelled to continue cutting its coat to a constantly diminishing cloth, with the result, again, that in respect of national efficiency, we shall cease to be able to maintain, for example, even the indispensable minimum of national and still less, of course, of Imperial defence. Taking the axiom for granted that rates and taxes are the only source upon which the State can draw in payment for its services, one if not both of the foregoing alternatives is inescapable; and a major problem of modern statesmanship is thus the discovery of a new and hitherto untapped source of the means of public expenditure.

The familiar illustration of the difference between the value produced by ten men working separately and the same ten working in co-ordination will perhaps serve to indicate the direction in which we must look for this new untapped source. The collective Wages, Salaries, Dividends and Profits that constitute the present financial income of the nation represent only the individual earnings of the ten men of our illustration taken separately. But their joint product, thanks to their association as a nation, with its rich heritage of means and culture, is vastly greater in value (as it is also in Price) than any sum defrayable merely by their individual earnings, the difference, in fact, being roughly the difference between the sum and the multiple of a series of numbers. And it is precisely to this increment due to association and not now paid to any individual that the State must look not only for its future expenditure (including National Dividends on the collective patrimony and enterprise), but for the means to the remission of all existing "taxation for revenue". A competent National Treasury, in full control of the national monetary system, could without the smallest difficulty begin tomorrow the progressive diminution of taxation and simultaneously the progressive increase of its expenditure on public services.

II 7

If it is true—as, of course, it is—that the Banks proper can create Money, are indeed, the creators of all the Money that exists now or at any given moment; and if, further-more, it be asked upon what ultimate "collateral" the Banks create and issue new Money—it will be found that the margin for the creation of "new money" is just as wide as the difference between Actual Consumption and Potential Production; in other words, that the source of Money for public expenditure is *not* confined to the pockets of those who have it (actual consuming power), but includes, and as its major part, the unutilized resources of real Production (potential consuming power). The sum of the actual incomes of the nation represents and can purchase, in fact, only a fraction of the real Wealth of the nation. And by doing exactly what the Banks do when they issue loans, make overdrafts, and buy Gold or Securities—namely, create new Money upon the "collateral" of the nation's unutilized productive resources—the "Treasury" could "finance" Public Expenditure without calling upon its citizens individually to sacrifice a penny of their present incomes. It will take some time yet, however, before any Chancellor of the Banks' appointment will be able to "see" the point; and, in the meanwhile, the nation will be like men in a boat hoarding their cans of drinking-water and fighting each other for them (with the State, at the instigation of the Banks, robbing them all) on a fresh-water lake as large as Superior and constantly growing larger.   II 3

The Budget

A generation or more will be necessary to bring home to the public mind the criminal absurdity of the system under which we now exist; but in the meantime an increasing number of people, who will shortly be strong enough to initiate action, are becoming convinced that the principles of the present Budget cannot long continue to be even workable. On the broad ground that it is monstrous that the sovereign nation, the ultimate source of all credit, should have to go cap in hand to its creature, the Bank of

England, and deposit collateral (in the form of tax-warrants) for overdraughts upon itself, just as if it were one of its own citizens, the fundamental principle of the present Budget is a perversion of common sense. But even allowing that the superstition of "Sound Finance" may continue to dominate mediocre minds, the actual operation of its machinery is bound to become progressively more and more difficult. If reason does not lie, the annual earned income of the nation, derived on account of human services individually rendered to current Production, must necessarily diminish relatively to the total collective Wealth of the nation *pari passu* with the displacement of human by solar energy; and since the expenditure of the State must, at the same time, necessarily increase with its Wealth, there is manifestly an inherent and ultimately fatal contradiction in the present principle of individual taxation. Properly regarded, all State expenditure, including the expenditure represented by the National Debt, is a National Capital Cost that should be more than balanced by the National Appreciation due to it. Assuming that the State were credited with the appreciation due to its expenditure, the result would be that every tax-payment would be in the nature of an investment upon which the taxpayers could draw a dividend. The more the taxes the greater the dividend. The banks, however, are at present the beneficiaries of the collective appreciation; and it is not to be expected that they will release their hold on the Budget without a struggle. V 2

The Treasury

It remains an enigma why our Treasury, that is alone finally responsible for the nation's financial policy— both domestic and foreign—alone escapes criticism or even intelligent comment. The "hidden hand" is reputed to extend from the "City", but the voice of its director is undoubtedly that of His Majesty's Treasury Lords at Whitehall. Our criticisms of the Banks, the City, and even Mr. Montagu Norman, are always tempered by the reflection that, after all, powerful by monopoly as they are, their monopoly is subject to the control of the Crown and Parliament through the agency of the accredited and paid State officials of the Treasury. Mr. Norman and his fraternity may well protest that they not only do no more than they are authorized to do, but that, if their policy is deemed anti-national, the Treasury must either approve or be incompetent; and, in any case, the relations of the City are with the Treasury and not with the nation at large. From the same point of view, it is obvious that whatever influences the City may bring to bear on the Treasury to shape the nation's policy, it is the Treasury at last that is responsible for it; no excuse will lie that the "City" determined it. Moreover, it is as obviously true of members of Parliament as of the members of any other corporation that they are finally controlled by the power of the purse; in other words, that even Parliament is much what the Treasury likes to make it; so that, in the end, the conclusion is forced on the objective observer that it is the Treasury that governs England and, in the particular case, is responsible for the present situation of the American Debt. Is there any means of bringing the Treasury to book or must we wait for catastrophe to settle accounts? Mr. Lloyd George has revealed how the ancient dug-ins at the Admiralty and War Office nearly lost us the war. As a matter of fact, the war was won by amateurs in every department. It is clear that the greater war of Real Plenty against Financial Scarcity is being lost to us on every field. Our relations with every nation, including our own

Dominions, are steadily growing worse as the Treasury strives to balance the Budget on obsolete principles. It is more than time that the personnel of the Treasury were told to get on or get out. V 8

ECONOMIC NATIONALISM, FREE TRADE, & FOREIGN INVESTMENT

The Liberal Tradition in Economics

The Budget can be balanced and kept balanced only by means that ensure precisely the opposite of a national revival of trade, namely, the artificial strangulation of the one absolutely free market the nation still possesses—its Home market. Upon any theory you like to proceed, assuming goodwill and not enmity to the people of England, the world-depression brought about by the inability of other nations to buy or borrow our goods would seem to call for the compensatory act of increased Home consumption. Because we are investing less abroad—in other words, exporting fewer goods in return for bonds—therefore we should have more to consume at home; and hence the primary policy of truly national statesmen in these circumstances would be to distribute purchasing power at home as fast as it was ceasing to be exported abroad. Not so, however, our National Government. Every other nation in the world must be restored to prosperity before our own; and if the worst comes to the worst and other nations cannot be restored, then our own nation must continue to suffer in empathetic self-denial.

II 3

The Budget, together with the tariffs that are now a settled factor in our national economy, has the disadvantage of its mixed parentage. By Protection out of Free Trade is not a pedigree that promises a great deal for the human race.

An end has been put to the practice, and soon will be put to the doctrine, of Free Trade, and consequently, if more slowly, to that ideal of Internationalism which has never been more in reality than a bankers' dream of power. The internationalism of which the best minds of the race have dreamed has never been the bankers' internationalism, based, as that is, on the disintegration of every nation and ultimately upon the extinction of nationality in the interests of a central-ized world-government composed of self-elected supermen of finance; but, in their simple minds, upon the voluntary co-operation for world-purposes of free peoples, that is to say, of nations at least mainly if not entirely self-sufficing. Within the Tariff walls now erected, it is possible, as it never could be under Free Trade, to proceed to set our own national house in order and to develop our home market by the adoption of Protection for the individual. This is not only a possible, it is an urgent and perhaps obligatory policy. Certainly if it is true, as it appears to be, that International trade is rapidly and surely diminishing never to be restored to its earlier importance, the significance of the home-market, even from the purely economic point of view, is easily doubled. And if a home-supply that has hitherto been suffi-cient to meet both a foreign and a home demand must pro-gressively be confined to the home-demand alone, *either* the present sabotage of our productive equipment must be car-ried to barbarous lengths, *or* some means must be found of distributing purchasing-power at home without requiring an export for its excuse or a rise in prices. As the means of the latter are now well known, we may hope that, before the necessity arises, when it will be too late, the institution of a National Dividend will have taken place.   I I

The Cobden tradition dies but it never surrenders; and at a recent meeting of the Memorial Association the Creed of the Founder was solemnly repeated: a Free Trade world and the absorption of the unemployed (the compulsorily leisured class) by an ever-expanding Foreign Trade. Certainly, if never before, faith is now needed to sustain Cobden's remaining disciples, since nowhere in the world today is Free Trade in operation; and the outlook for the absorption of the unemployed by any probable or even possible extension of Foreign Trade, that is to say, of Exports, is one of blank despair. Apart from the fact that Free Trade may be said to have done its work of industrializing the world, the conditions under which Exports in the past have been encouraged have now decisively changed for the worse. Exports in excess of Imports, or the famous favourable Balance of Trade, have always been obtained in the past by Foreign investment. That is to say we have not actually been selling foreign nations our goods, but lending them the means, first of all, to dispense with our goods and, ultimately, to compete with us in the rest of the world's markets. The Americans have a phrase for it: they call it "Suicide Traffic". And now the disclosure is beginning to be made that all the time we have been impoverishing our own people to lend to strangers, we have been lending to nations that could not afford to borrow and have not the means to repay. It is still, of course, true that England could have enough Foreign Trade tomorrow to absorb all the four millions of our unemployed. By extending loans to every needy or greedy nation conditional upon the loans being spent with us, we could undoubtedly make our factories hum as they did during the War. But the "trade" in return, except in the form of raw material to keep us at it, would consist practically entirely of promises to pay which even then would in the end be repudiated. Short of this expedient, which even the "City" is not now likely to adopt, there is literally no prospect of the revival of Foreign Trade.

International Trade

There is nothing fundamentally wrong with the existing machinery of international trade and commerce. There is even, from our point of view, nothing fundamentally wrong with either its diminishing amount or its distribution. The problem before the Empire and the World, in fact, is neither an Imperial nor a World-problem primarily, but a domestic problem, common to all nations, of home-distribution. The world's money-problem can and must be settled first at home and only afterwards internationally. It is not of the smallest use to attempt to settle the money-problem Imperially or by Sterling area. Each such area, when it is formed, will only find itself in antagonism and possibly in sharp conflict with the excluded areas. The only area in which Monetary-reform can be safely and effectively begun is the area domestic of every single sovereign economic unit. When one nation of the world has the courage to reform its own internal monetary-system without waiting on the By your Leave of any Imperial or Sterling or World Conference, World-reform and the salvation of Civilization will have begun.   I 4

And Money

It is possible only on paper to devise a Monetary system that shall command the assent of competing sovereign nations; in practice any such scheme would break down in a week. It is assumed quite mistakenly that the pre-War Gold Standard was a matter of agreement among nations; but the evidence is now tragically complete that it was never devised but grew up, and that no nation or group of nations could, in fact, lay down its rules or punish any brach of them. A nation's Money is like an individual's money. A nation may be willing to spend it, invest it, give it away or keep it locked up, but what no nation will ever do (except, alas, to its own nationals) is to confide the control of its Monetary system to another nation or to any group of nations. The inference from this indisputable fact is clear. Every nation claims and must be allowed the right to regulate its own Monetary system *internally*, and as regards its external Money arrangements, to be free to enter or not to enter any Sterling or Imperial or World convention at its discretion. It is true that as yet no nation has even begun to set its own domestic Money-system in order. Every domestic money-system is under the paramount influence if not complete control of a World-system which, in one sense happily, has now broken down. The problem before every nation today is to arrange its domestic money economy to its own satisfaction, before its arch-enemy, an international Gold control, recovers its breath and once again subordinates every nation to what the Pope has described as "the accursed hunger for Gold". The breakdown of the Gold Standard and of Free Trade—parts of one whole—gives every nation a breathing space for the recapture of its soul. Once, however, that Gold is re-admitted, even under the courtesy title of Sterling, as the arbiter of domestic currencies, each nation will again have failed to save its own soul and the world will be lost into the bargain.   I 6

And the Nation

The Internationalism now in favour would only intensify the existing economic misery of the world. Production no doubt has profited by the division and specialization of individual labour and by the division and specialization of national areas; and it stands to reason that Production as such would benefit by the application of the principle of the division of labour and function to all the nations of the world. But apart from the question whether the sacrifice of the wholeness of the individual has not been too high a price to pay (assuming it even to have been a necessary price, which we deny) for increased production, there can be no doubt whatever that the problem before the world today is the problem of Distribution and not of Production, and that a further increase in the world's ability to Produce would, in the absence of the discovery of a corresponding means of Distribution, simply raise the scale of the existing crisis. But how is the problem of Distribution to be solved? What is the most promising area for its experimental trial? It cannot, in our judgment, be at either of the extremes of the social series. The individual is too small for it and the world too big for it. The problem of Distribution, in fact, can be tackled and solved neither by an individual return to a state of nature nor by the Utopianism of a World-State, but by one of the existing living and evolving economic units called nations.   I 21

And Markets

The ability to export, in terms of a surplus of production over consumption, is increasing simultaneously in every industrialized country, that is, in fact, every country; and hence the world "market" for export must be diminishing at the same rate. Is it not obvious that unless each industrialized nation learns, and very soon, how to consume what it produces and to content itself with complementary and reciprocal international trade, the competition for markets—not for goods, but for investments—will become more and more fierce, until it breaks out into open war?   I 19

As other countries become industrialized—and even today there are no purely agricultural nations—they are bound to cease to offer a market for our manufactured goods. And since, thanks to our plain living and high thinking, our own manufacturing ability would continue also to increase along with theirs, the effect would be simply to intensify the existing situation; an exporting system expanding to infinity would still be trying to squeeze into an importing system contracting to zero. Even if we assume that by princely salesmanship on a pauper diet this country managed to capture the lion's share of the diminishing foreign trade still going, the first effect would be to put our weaker rivals out of business, the second to risk a conflict, no longer strictly commercial, with our more powerful rivals, and the ultimate effect to leave us still with the same increasing and indisposable surplus of productivity over exportability. I 6

The Lausanne Conference like many Conferences still to be held exhibited a prehistoric mentality which naturally confuses cause and effect. Because it *appears* that Tariffs and Embargoes, Restrictions and Quotas are causes of the decline of international trade, it is assumed that with their removal international trade would revive. But the simple and obvious fact is that Tariffs and all the rest of the restrictions upon international trade are designed to produce the very effect complained of—and in the interest of the increasing self-sufficiency of the nations concerned. Is it conceivable, for example, that America will abandon her high tariff policy because it restricts international trade? Agreed that it may restrict her own international trade as well as that of the rest of the world. But the exchange—for America—of her 98 per cent of domestic trade for the 2 per cent of her international trade is not to be thought of and, in fact, neither party in America dreams of advocating the reduction of the existing tariffs. What the argument we are advancing against the Lausanne and all similar Conferences amounts to is this: that, thanks to the spread of industrialism, every nation will erect tariffs as soon as possible and keep and raise them unless forcibly prevented. That international trade, apart from complementary exchanges, will inevitably diminish, is not only implicit in the fact, it will be the evidence that the Tariffs have answered their object.   I 13

The Decline of Foreign Trade

For the period immediately succeeding the invention of machinery and the discovery of the use of coal, there was a plausible excuse for the ambition of a pioneer manufacturing country like England first to get the world into its debt and then to live happily ever after on the interest. But quite inevitably and exactly to the degree that the romantic policy was effective in distributing machinery, it was bound to come to a dead end; and, in fact, by 1927 the total possible Foreign Trade of the world, dependent upon Foreign loans, reached its maximum. Even in that peak year, however, the Foreign trade of the leading manufacturing countries of the world was only a fraction of its total trade. English Foreign Trade, for instance, was in 1927 only a quarter of its total trade; and, in the case of America, with an output ability of one-third the whole world's production, its foreign trade in that year, even reckoning in its reciprocal exchange, was only one-twentieth of its total trade. In other words, English domestic trade was three times, and American domestic trade was nineteen times, its foreign trade even in the year when foreign trade was at its historic maximum. From 1927 onwards, as everybody now knows, there has not only been a decline in foreign trade, but the decline has been progressive. In 1931, the total foreign trade of the world was only a quarter of its amount in 1927; in 1933 it was about one-eighth. It is still dropping. Is there anybody in possession of his normal senses who imagines that 1927 or anything like it can ever return on the dial of the world?   III 2

It is perfectly possible for any single industrial nation to create a favourable balance of trade for itself by simply exporting more than it imports; but it is obviously not possible for all nations to do the same. And again, it is perfectly possible for a single country to procure the lowering and even the abolition of tariffs against itself by the simple device of never requiring either the repayment of foreign loans or the payment of any interest on them. But since the maintenance of the present financial system and, above all, the exploitation of the home market, absolutely require both that every nation shall strive for a favourable balance of trade, and, at the same time, be paid, not in Goods but in Money (or credit Gold) for the difference, every nation is sooner or later forced to pursue simultaneously two quite incompatible objectives—a free market in the rest of the world for its exports and a closed market at home for imports.   II 4

Economic Independence of Nations
        The first condition, or rather, the last, of equality of nations is not political independence, though it may precede the other, but economic independence; and the stamp and seal of economic independence is that a nation shall be in sovereign control of its own financial credit, and be dependent for its domestic money-system neither upon a foreign authority nor upon a private monopoly in its own midst.
                    III 2

The Mirage of the World State

To minds corrupted in the school of mere words presided over by Mr. H. G. Wells and his kind, the appeal of "International Co-operation" is irresistible in the same degree that its actual implications are ignored. It is possible, of course, by stretching the meanings of words, to pretend that between a world of economic democracies reciprocally exchanging their products and a world in "international co-operation", there is little or no difference. But the difference, it will be confirmed on reflection, is the whole difference between a world of free and independent nations in voluntary economic and political relationship and a world still nominally composed, perhaps, of nations, but actually under the dictatorship of a super-State consisting of the group of individuals for whose benefit the world-corporation would be controlled. It is little short of stupefying, indeed, to find men like Mr. Wells, whose expressed opinion of the ability of national bankers is properly contemptuous, nevertheless prepared to entrust the government of a nation-less world to an absolute committee of financiers. Is it within the range of even astronomical probability that men who by their type and function have obtained and now exercise complete control over their own nations, and *deny them the use of their own resources*, will, when presented with the world to exploit for power, suddenly become benevolent and samurai? We affirm that under cover of the appealing and popular phrase of International Co-operation nothing less than the will to world-power of national bankers, tired of merely national counters, is being pursued; and, moreover, that no less momentous an issue is at stake than the future of the world perhaps for ever.

The situation of the world at this moment is clearly this:

a few creditor countries, America, England, have more Money owing to them than their debtor nations can pay in Money, or are permitted to pay in Goods. Not only therefore are the latter bankrupt, but their creditors, with nobody else to lend to, are equally distressed since they no longer have any use for their surplus money, being like Moneylenders, whose clients are all sunk in debt and whose assets are worthless. Between which of these categories of nations, we ask, is international co-operation to take place? We can conceive the co-operation of the debtors to default as a body; we can conceive, but with more difficulty, the co-operation of the creditors to distrain on the estates of the debtors and divide the proceeds amicably. But what we find it impossible to conceive is that from either course the prosperity of any nation, debtor or creditor, is likely to ensue. Like the dead-weight of internal debts, the dead weight of internation debts is past bearing, and since both debts are owing ultimately to the same group of individuals, namely, the manipulators of the Central Banks of the World, there is only one possibility of genuine international co-operation. It is for nations, individually but simultaneously, to recover the control of their money-systems from the "Cities" that have filched it from them and thereafter to use their Money for the Production, Exchange and Distribution of Goods.

Tariffs are justified only to the degree that the equivalent of the goods they exclude is distributed at home. If our own people have not sufficient purchasing-power to absorb their own production, it is no remedy for the defect to exclude foreign production, since it simply leaves more glaring the disparity between domestic prices and domestic purchasing-power.   III 4

Let us suppose that the age of miracles is still with us, and that the results of a World Conference surpass even the dreams of its authors. We will suppose, in fact, that on each of five main subjects of discussion the assembled financial authorities not only arrive at agreed conclusions but at conclusions they have the power and the will to put into effect. In as brief a period as possible the price-level of primary commodities is raised, exchanges are stabilized, the Gold Standard is restored, all the existing International debts are cancelled or scaled down to tolerable levels, and the world of nations is rapidly steered in the direction of complete Free Trade. Let us throw into the bargain, since we are giving miracles away, that the World is completely disarmed save for a police force, that a single Monetary system prevails over the globe, and that nothing except local manners and customs distinguishes one nation from another. We hope it will be agreed that in this presentation of the case for the authors of the Conference we are omitting nothing that they could desire. And if, on the other hand, there is anything wanting in our fulfilment of their wildest dreams, they have only to mention it to have it allowed. But what, we then ask, is to be expected of a world, framed to their heart's desire, that we are not already familiar with in the model upon which we have constructed it? Such a world, it is obvious, is only the United States writ large in nations in place of states. As everybody must surely see, America is already the realized epitome of the World-State of which the Central Bankers and their agents dream. It is true that America is for the moment only 98 per cent self-sufficient while a World-State would presumably be 100 per cent self-sufficient. But can it be said that a 2 per cent difference of self-sufficiency invalidates our parallel and makes it certain or even probable that a United States of the World would succeed where the United States of America has failed?

If, save for 2 per cent, and that very doubtful, America does, in fact, embody and illustrate the ideal of the World Conference in respect of all and more of the agreed conclusions to which the Conference could conceivably arrive, is it reasonable to suppose that even the impossible success of the Conference would produce in practice anything very different from the condition of affairs in its smaller model and pattern? We shall not live to see it, nor will any now living, but as surely as the World-State of present-day aspiration, stimulated by International Finance, is brought into actual existence—if ever—so surely will the phenomena now visible in America be repeated but on a vaster scale. In all the plans, proposals and even benevolent intentions of the World Conference there is not one single hope for the solution of the problem that has reduced America to its present plight and the rest of the world with it, the problem of the distribution, nationally or internationally, of Plenty.   III 9

To attempt to make of the British Commonwealth a second and a rival United States is not only doomed to failure but to failure from the start. For better or for worse, the very principle of the Commonwealth is opposed to its development as a centralized Federation. What is needed is not the organization of the Commonwealth from above—that is to say, under the direction of its Central Banks—but from its parts by voluntary association. And the first step towards this is the restoration of financial sovereignty to the people of each constituent dominion.   III 19

Epidemic Default on International Debts
        The increasing unwillingness culminating, when pressed, into absolute refusal to pay debts internationally incurred, marks the end of an era—the era of International

Moneylending. "An immense volume of international trade," *The Times* says, "has in the past been secured by lending money to customers" (that is, on credit); and with the present defaults it is practically certain that this form of "investment" has come to an end. The question is: What is to take the place formerly occupied by this Export market? In what is the money of the Banks to be invested when all credit-worthy foreign demand for it has ceased? And what is to become of the profits of the exporting Industrialists, the International financiers, and the Shipping interests who have hitherto battened on Foreign Trade Credits—to say nothing of the Labour employed on Goods for Export? It is useless to suggest that an adequate substitute for our disappearing "Foreign Trade" can be found in commercial "investment" in the Home market. Though it may be true that most of the recent "recovery" is due to an increase in Home, and not in Foreign, demand, it would be a mistake to expect that recovery can be maintained by this means under the existing system. And the reasons for this are simple. In the first place, unlike Foreign investment loans which, in effect, are non-repayable (as we are now discovering), Home loans are not only expected to be repaid, but the debtors can be distrained upon—facts that ensure both reluctance to incur loans and a very "liquid" policy as to their use. (Only bank-run concerns will, in all probability, in future either venture to raise loans or be allowed to control their management.) And in the second place, by reason of the very fact that domestic loans and investments, whether made by individuals, corporations or the State itself (in the form of Public Works) are actually repayable, the present disparity between Prices and Incomes will be enlarged by at least twice the amount of our former Foreign investment. You cannot, financially, get out of a market more than you put in; and a repayable loan is not actually put in. It appears, no doubt, to be put in when it is distributed as Wages, etc.; and it actually adds to immediate purchasing-power. But since it only does so by creating a debt, that is to say, a claim on the future, the appearance of a net addition to purchasing-power over a period of time is completely illusory. We have seen that in the case of Foreign Investments they have added to the purchasing-power of the borrowers only by being, in fact if not in theory, non-repayable. In short, they have been a free gift. Unless, therefore, Home "investment" takes the same form, namely, that of a free gift, the more of it the worse. The least that it will mean is that the Home market will get into debt instead of the Foreign market; and, in the end, what was denied as a gift will be taken by bankruptcy.

V 12

Foreign v. Domestic Investment

Everybody of "City" mentality is distressed to know how to provide the home market with purchasing-power in the absence of its creation by means of foreign investment. And it is certainly true that without a special creation and distribution of purchasing-power for home-Consumption, the decline in Foreign Investment will leave the nation additionally short of purchasing-power by the amount that has hitherto been exported. But the "remedy" for the defect of purchasing power thus exposed is not to attempt the impossible, namely, the restoration of the policy of Foreign Investment, but to adopt the policy of domestic Investment in increased domestic Consumption.

V 2

Foreign Investment (we do *not* mean Foreign Trade or the interchange of Goods) impoverishes both the country that borrows and the country that lends. Of the borrowing country it makes a debtor who grows to hate its creditor more and more; and of the lending country it makes a creditor who can only continue "prosperous" by throwing good money after bad. If the default of foreign creditors under the auspices of the League of Nations will discourage to zero point all Foreign Investment as such, there is the better hope that nations will learn, under necessity, how to live on their own resources, the simple truth being that a nation whose credit is good enough to borrow on has a credit good enough to bank on for itself.

It is obvious that when credit is lent abroad it must be implemented with either Goods or Gold; and it is equally obvious that both the interest on the loans and their final repayment (if ever made) must be paid in one or both of the same media. But what is to happen if (a) we do not stock the Goods in demand and must therefore export Gold; or (b) payment of interest or repayment of the loan cannot be made in Gold but only in Goods? We have, in the first instance, parted with our Gold (with the effect of dislocating our internal Monetary system) and we are offered in return Goods which our financial system does not permit us to welcome. In these circumstances there appears only one thing to be done, namely, to reinvest the interest as it accrues, as the only means of even appearing to be repaid. And this, in fact, is what has been happening over the last quarter of a century, with the result that the "City" has today foreign loans to its "credit" of over 5000 millions, on which it is doubtful whether a net penny has ever been actually paid in either Gold or Goods. All, in fact, that the nation has to show for this enormous export is a portfolio of bonds, held in the "City", on which even the interest is paid only by the aid of further loans. But it is precisely *this* form of Foreign Trade that is in question when the myriad-headed

M

"City", that is, less than 1 per cent of the population, talks of Foreign Trade. The "City" has, of course, no use for Goods as such and equally, of course, is aware that the debts of the world are hundreds of times more than the Gold of the world. But by exporting Credit (the nation's Credit) on the mortgages of foreign borrowers, the "City" can delude itself and the silly people that its moneylending business is genuine Foreign Trade, when, in fact, even the Interest is non-collectable.

The upshot of the matter is that no nation in control of its own monetary system has any need to lend or to borrow from other nations. Foreign Trade among sovereign credit nations would increasingly approximate to the theoretical ideal of complementary exchange or none at all.   I 24

An External Currency

An external currency or, rather, money of account, for conducting exchanges between nations, is by no means necessarily dependent either upon the internal Monetary system or upon the value of its internal unit. It would be perfectly possible, indeed, for any nation to accept and conform to a general standard in all foreign transactions while retaining complete freedom to regulate its own domestic money-arrangements. Let us suppose, for instance, that in our own domestic economy we employed our Money-system merely as a means of regulating Production and Distribution—as a system of realistic book-keeping for the resources and needs of the commonwealth, in short—would it be beyond the wit of man to maintain the two systems, each in its own sphere, simultaneously and without prejudice one to the other? It is obvious that Communist Russia, even if the problem is there very imperfectly solved, has at least succeeded in separating the two functions of Money, Money for internal use and Money for foreign exchange; and surely what Communist Russia can do, we with all our "experts" can do better. So far is it from being true that no nation can solve its own domestic problem without world-agreement, the very reverse is true: no world-agreement is now possible until at least one great nation has set its own internal money-system in civilized order.   I 5

The Fear of Economic Isolation

Nobody in his senses talks of absolute "economic isolation," but, at best, of effort towards it, as implying a progressive state of security and well-being. Furthermore, whether desirable or not, even whether likely to be disastrous or not, the fact stares the world in the face that nations, as they become industrialized, demand less and less of each other, with the consequence that they are more and more forced to try to live upon their own resources. Again, what is in truth at the back of this outcry against national self-sufficiency? Is it any more than the fear that our export trade is in danger? But this brings us to the domestic question of the distribution of our production, the essential feature of which, under the existing system, is that it is impossible to employ our own people, that is, to distribute purchasing power among them—except in payment, not for imports, but for exports, and, again, not for exports to balance our imports, but for exports in excess of our imports. In other words, when the Prime Minister and the rest speak of foreign trade as our "life-blood", they do not in the least mean merely the barter of goods of equal value. They mean the excess of our exports over our imports or what they call a "favourable balance of trade"; and it is precisely this, and not simple trade, that is in peril from the inability of nations to borrow and the unwillingness of nations to lend. So long as this is the condition of the world—and we see it as increasingly probable—foreign trade, together with all the shipping and transport auxiliaries, will continue to languish with no hope of revival. Until, if ever, we or America or France begin to lend our foreign customers the financial credit with which to go through the technical motions of appearing to buy from us, it is quite certain that our imports will continue to threaten to exceed our exports, until, in the end, presumably, they will, as they should, exactly balance.   I 5

The Remedy

Excellent as is the proposed policy of reciprocal and complementary balanced foreign trading it would be disastrous to block up what, in effect, has been hitherto a safety-valve for the escape of purchasing-power, without simultaneously creating an alternative device for its internal combustion or consumption. Unless, in fact, a means is adopted for the increase of domestic consumption by *at least* the amount hitherto exported in the form of foreign investment, then it is perfectly certain that either Production must progressively slow down almost to a standstill, or, if Production is maintained and, worse, increased, the boiler will burst and blow the whole present system to Communist or Fascist bits.   V 10

On the one hand, therefore, it is absolutely necessary that each nation should quickly learn how to conduct its domestic economy so as to make competition for Foreign Markets for Investment superfluous; and, on the other hand, it is equally necessary that notice be given to Wall Street and Lombard Street that their day is over. And steps, at the same time, should be taken to settle the question of International Debts once and for all either by a Jubilee of mutual cancellation or at least by writing them down and making them payable in Goods. We have no doubt whatever that by these measures not only the peace of the world could be assured indefinitely, but, better still, each and every nation would speedily be put in the enjoyment as well as in the nominal possession of all it could produce. V II

Foreign Trade and the City

Left to themselves, all the great houses of the City could scarcely run a whelk-stall, still less compete with real industrialists in modern industry. Their life-work—now as ever, from the earliest days of Moneylending—is to create, lend and regulate the supply of Money, the one indispensable commodity in every exchange of industrial commodities, to their own profit and power. We are not stating this as a revolutionary discovery but as a simple fact the existence and significance of which have been carefully concealed from the general public under the cloak of high finance. The City is a factory where Money is made. Money is in universal demand as no other commodity is. Its price is determined by the relation of its Supply to its Demand. By keeping it in short supply—by the operation called Deflation—the City manufacturers of Money can effectively control industry and, at their discretion, even buy and sell it. The fact, for instance, that eighty per cent of industry to-day is in possession of the City, whose great houses have never put any other commodity upon the market but Money that cost them nothing, is evidence of the effectiveness of their control; since it means, in simple language, that four-fifths of industry could be made "bankrupt" tomorrow if it suited the banks to call in their loans of costless but legalized credit. And it is to this industry, parasitic upon genuine industry, that the Treasury turns for advice in a crisis which the

City itself, consciously or unconsciously, has brought about.   I 5

Economic Nationalism

It is not practicable to stop half-way between a unitary World and a unitary Nation. Unity, like every other good thing, begins at home. Nations have tried to establish domestic prosperity by fetching a compass about the world and entangling all nations in the same net, and they have failed; there is not one prosperous nation in the world to-day. And fetching a compass about the Empire will similarly fail if it is tried. There is only one way to world-prosperity, to Empire unity, and ultimately to World-unity; it is the way of Economic Nationalism.   III 13

Economic Nationalism as formulated by List, continued in spirit by scores of his successors, and now technically in-strumented in the doctrines of Major Douglas, most em-phatically does not envisage a world of national Robinson Crusoes, each eking out a precarious living on its own island. On the contrary, what is envisaged in Economic Nationalism is the self-respecting economic independence of nations honestly engaged in reciprocal trade to their mutual advantage, but excluding the servile relationship of Debtor and Creditor. As it is a matter of common knowledge that all that the Central Banks care about is precisely the inter-national relationship of Debtor and Creditor—Money being the only commodity in which they deal—it is only to be expected that they should oppose and misrepresent Eco-nomic Nationalism since it is the only enemy they have to fear.   III 4

We do not advocate Economic Nationalism, we simply point to it as an emergent fact as unmistakable and as inevitable as the rise of political Nationalism after the final destruction of the first World-State, the Roman Empire. Furthermore we have never affirmed that Economic Nationalism, even when it reaches its full development, will either involve or entail the absurd condition or consequence now attributed to the doctrine by its interested enemies, namely, that it must mean an end to foreign trade, and the resignation of every nation to living exclusively upon its own local resources. All, in fact, that is specifically implied in the doctrine—apart, of course, from the actual conditions that have created it—is the resolution as well as the necessity of every nation to attain *financial* independence, that is to say, to be under no necessity either to lend or to borrow as a mere means of distributing enough domestic purchasing-power to buy the total domestic Production. It should be obvious, both from this definition and from the familiar facts at the back of it, that the only possible enemies of National Financial Independence are the people whose trade is in international indebtedness in terms of their own commodity of Money. To the plain citizen, to the whole army of actual producers, even to the creators of the "invisible exports" of services rendered abroad, it is not of the smallest concern that there should be a "favourable" balance of trade, in other words, a foreign loan of credit. All that is necessary to us who form at least ninety-nine point nine of the community is that the value of the goods imported shall be at least equal to the value of our exports; in short, that the exchange of real advantages shall be to our profit. But this unfortunately, is not in the least how our fractional percentage of the population, engaged in the City, look upon the matter. Money being their monopoly by Royal licentiousness, and moneylending being their only trade, their interest is neither in the mere exchange of Goods nor, still less, in the reciprocal advantages to the actual traders. Their interest is only in the *difference* between Exports and Imports, and equally in an unfavourable or favourable difference, since either involves a resort to their own commodity of Money as Credit or as Debt. It is this International Finance —as it is called—that really lies at the bottom (or, rather, next to the bottom) of all the international troubles of the world today; and although, in truth, every nation could become and wishes to become financially independent, the conspiracy of the international financiers, with their headquarters in every Central Bank, with London at their head, will not let them.   IV 12

Economic nationalism is not a theory or merely an ideal arising in the study of the political theorist; it is a diagnosis of the direction of inexorable facts. And unless nations can learn to live without taking in each other's washing and turn to doing their own, it is certain that their economic linen will be dirty. The need to export, we repeat, is an artificial need, created by the simple fact that at present no community can purchase its own production. We have only to create and distribute sufficient purchasing-power in every community to enable the community to utilize its own productive resources to the full in order to reduce the present fever of foreign competition and avoid the intermittent fits of war.   I 12

Thanks to the universalization of the mechanical technique that originated in this country, the nations of the world, even before the war, were well on the way to self-sufficiency in respect of secondary if not of primary products.

The virtual blockade of nations which the war entailed put some additional touches on the process previously begun. The longer the war lasted the more self-sufficient domestically the various nations were bound to try to become. The establishment after the war in every country of tariffs, for the crazy purpose of balancing budgets to oblige banks, put the finishing touches on the whole process, so that today, at a pinch, there is scarcely a nation that could not and does not feel anxious to support itself, if only as a wise insurance against a not impossible future and more terrible World-war. Economic nationalism, defined as the pursuit of national self-sufficiency, is not the mad whim of a world gone mad. As a matter of fact, it is not in the least incompatible with internationalism as distinct from the diabolical doctrine of super-nationalism. In view of all the circumstances, actual and contingent, a statesman today who is not nationalist in economics, and internationalist only in politics, is at best behind the times and at worst a danger to his country. And in an island such as our own, the danger is appalling.   I 15

Economic Nationalism, left at the mercy of a Financial system designed for Economic Internationalism, will not only fail to deliver the latter's goods, but, as a policy, it is the straight and short road, both to national bankruptcy in terms of money, and to national impoverishment in terms of real wealth. The present Financial system actually if not avowedly is designed for one grand objective—maximum potential domestic Production and minimum actual domestic Consumption, with a view to the creation of a maximum "surplus" financially controlled, and available, therefore, for lending either abroad or at home. In the defect of a domestic demand for loans from this "surplus" for the purposes of new Capital Production, there is literally (under the system) no other outlet for the surplus than Foreign investment. And in the absence of Foreign Investment as a means of escape and exit for the "surplus", not only is the "surplus" retained at home in idleness (as its financial controllers say), but (and this is the practical point) the nation at large cannot possibly draw upon it for the simple reason that there is no demand for their employment to replace it, or any other means available for procuring the purchasing-power with which to make use of it. Foreign Investment (or an excess of Exports over Imports; or, equally, the export of the aforesaid "surplus") is thus under the existing system, a safety-valve without the free working of which it is inevitable that the whole present economic machine must cool down, blow up or be re-adapted. Cooling down is brought about by prolonged deflation as blowing up is brought about by prolonged inflation. But, on the other hand, to escape from either of these consequences by resuming Foreign Investment is simply to restore the old conditions in even more unfavourable circumstances. There is one adaptation necessary and one only—to devise an internal Consumption mechanism that shall distribute purchasing-power at home at the same rate (at least) as the rate at which it could be invested abroad if the Foreign market were both infinitely absorbent and completely credit-worthy. The means to this domestic safety-valve to replace the dangerous safety-valve of Foreign investment is the National Dividend and the Compensated Retail Price. Without these, Economic Nationalism is simply sitting on the present safety-valve and suffering the consequences.   IV 21

Economic Nationalism is only a convenient name for the economic phenomena now common to most countries and manifested as an increasing tendency on the part of each to become, in fact, less and less dependent upon foreign countries. And all that we have added to it is the practical suggestion that in the event (which appears to us inevitable) that this tendency continues, under the combined influence of Invention, International Debts and the fear of another World-war, it will sooner or later be necessary to adapt our domestic Financial system to it by providing for the domestic market an additional purchasing-power at least as great as the amounts we have hitherto been able to export. That the adoption of any such means must inevitably entail the resumption by the nation of control over its own money we do not, of course, deny. The private Monopoly of the production, distribution and exchange of the nation's purchasing-power must certainly be brought to an end. But that a nation that has in a generation exported thousands of millions worth of Goods in excess of its Imports cannot live upon its own resources (balancing Exports and Imports) is simply nonsense.   IV 23

The League of Nation's statistical experts are not convinced that the Depression is normal and as good as over already. Without wringing the world's withers, the League experts nevertheless remark that the *total* of international trade, in 1934, one half of its 1929 magnitude, shows no sign of rapid increase. One or two competitors in the world-shambles have been temporarily disabled, leaving the rest to profit by their absence, but, on the whole, the aggregate quantity of international trade shows less and less evidence of expanding with the various national means of Production. It is flogging a dead horse to attempt to restore the Gold Standard as a means to the restoration of International trade. In the first place, the Gold Standard is never going to be restored. And, in the second place, Gold Standard or no, the world is a different world today; and most unmistakably it is not the world of International finance, but a world of increasing and determined Economic Nationalism.   V 25

The League of Nations

A Federation cannot be stable whose members consist of slaves and free men in the political sense; but it is a thousand times more to the point that a Federation cannot be stable whose members consist of debtors and creditors. All the statesmen of nineteenth century ideas are still under the impression that friendly co-operation between individuals, classes and nations, is possible upon merely judicial grounds. Provided that each of the parties recognizes the complete equality of all the rest, it is only a matter of reason to get them to agree. The fact, however, is that the establishment of debtor-creditor relations between equals at once destroys their equality and introduces an element of discord that is all the more malignant because it cannot be objected to. We affirm with all the emphasis at our command that, without a previous settlement of the question of international indebtedness, and a resolution thereafter to incur no more of it, any new League of Nations, even if it should ever come into being, will fail as completely as the Versailles League. Quite inevitably it will break up into groups, if not of Victors and Vanquished, then of desperate Debtors and callous Creditors.   IV 9

Never from the outset was it conceivable that a League of Victors and Vanquished, Creditors and Debtors, should endure. Only a League of free and independent nations has the slightest chance of permanence. The evil trail of International Finance, in the palpable disguise of the Bank for International Settlements, was from the first calculated to poison the air for concord. Nor could a super-State of bankers' bailiffs be expected to ensure the peaceful disarmament of the world. IV 1

The economic interrelationships which led the National Leaguers to believe that the political federation of the world was feasible, were the result, not of genuine reciprocal needs arising amongst equals, but of the Imperialist exploitation of a dominant Power; and exactly to the degree that the component nations of the premature League began to realize the involuntary nature of their union and to acquire the economic means of independence, they have tended to disperse. The failure of the League of Nations, in other words, is not the failure of the human spirit to seek peace and ensue it; but it is due to the refusal of nations to tolerate a forced marriage when the honourable estate of voluntary co-operation appears now to be possible. V 1

Assume that the League of Nations represented an effort to unify the world under the ægis of an International Money Monopoly operating through the Bank for International Settlements; and assume again (as we may) that this attempt has failed. Since it is not in the nature of Power to abdicate or to cease to endeavour to extend itself, we may confidently look for the renewal of the effort in another direction. But in what direction? Suppose that, in the interval, the Central Banks of the various Powers, having realized their inability to control the world openly, through Basle and Geneva, should have disguised themselves as sovereign States and, with a popular dictator as their unconscious agent and tool, should then have proceeded to control, first, his domestic Monetary policy "in the name of the State", and, afterwards, his international Money policy, "in the name of peace"—

would not many things, now puzzling, appear relatively clear—to say nothing of events still to come? The following lights, it appears to us, would begin to be thrown upon the world's darkness. The identity of the domestic financial and economic policy of the various dictators would be explained. Their efforts to limit armaments among themselves, irrespective of merely national feelings, would become intelligible; likewise their efforts to pool spheres of financial interest—witness the otherwise incomprehensible exertions of our own "City" to finance Japanese and any other foreign "competitors". Again, the plea of Germany (blurted out in her usual naïve way) that she was under the impression that the rest of the Powers *wanted* her to suppress Jews and Communists is evidence that collusion between dictators is at least instinctive if not yet rationalized; for what is more probable than that if nations revolted against the League of Nations, classes will revolt against a League of Dictators? To end our speculations it is significant that since Germany administered the *coup de grace* to the League of Nations—rapprochements of the most surprising kind have taken place between all the dictatorial Powers, including the untouchable Red Russia and the unspeakable Yellow Japan. IV 25

Japan

There is simply not enough purchasing-power distributed in the home market to make an effective demand for more than a diminishing fraction of our domestic Production; with the necessary and logical consequence that either (*a*) more purchasing-power must be distributed at home and by other means than by the creation of Debt, or (*b*) purchasing-power for export must be manufactured and given to foreigners on condition that they spend it

in our domestic market. But since the method (*a*) of supplementing the deficiency of domestic purchasing-power
would have the apparently criminal effect of enabling the
community to Consume its own Production, the method
(*b*) must be pursued even when, as now, it threatens to
become as bloody as it is already idiotic. To look for "markets for investment"—that is, in plain language, for foreigners
to whom to give the means of employing Englishmen
—was in the good old altruistic Imperial days, a pastime for
Bellmen, with an occasional sight of the Snark for reward.
But in these days of rapid progression everywhere in the
direction of Economic Nationalism (again in plain language,
the repudiation of past and the disinclination to incur future
foreign debts) the search for foreign markets for Investment
is much more likely to flush a Boojum than a Snark. Take,
for instance, the dispatch of the expedition of the Federation
of British Industries to Manchukuo for the discovery of
holes in which to bury the products of British labour (of
course, under the plea that only by exports can the British
nation live on what it produces)—the consequences of this
ill-advised adventure may easily be incalculably tragical for
the people of this country. In the first place, the tacit recognition of the conquest of Manchukuo by Japanese Imperialism is a body-blow to any prospective authority of the
League of Nations. In the second place, even though
America and Germany are for the moment down and out,
their recovery in the end is certain; and their discovery of
the fact that England has shared the spoils with Japan in
their absence will certainly not conduce to their friendliness
to us. Thirdly, we wonder whether the F.B.I. ever even
look beyond their noses, and ask themselves what the
"Empire" will think on seeing them equipping an Asiatic
power for the exclusion of colonial goods. Finally, does it

never occur to these patriotic Judases that after selling their own people for yen, they may find that even the thirty pieces are denied them; in short, that, when she can, Japan will dispense with their services in the whole of Eastern Asia? We are not writing without the book when we say that the expedition of the F.B.I. in search of fields for the investment of "City" money created consternation among England's friends. And their consternation was equalled if not surpassed by the disgust among those who are aware that the only real motive of the expedition was to maintain the existing financial system and to stave off the day when the British nation can enjoy its own Production.   V 17-21

Japan stands belatedly in the position today in which England stood a hundred and fifty years ago; and is as little likely as we were then to consent to the restriction of her "Imperial" future without prolonged struggle. On the face of it, the petition of Lancashire, once the sturdy champion of world-competition and the devil take the hindmost, to come to terms with Japanese manufacturers not only in the Empire but all over the world, is an admission of weakness if not of defeat from the start. And there is much to be said—and Lancashire has long ago said it!—for Japan's disinclination to desist from the pursuit of victory. If Japan has succeeded in ousting Lancashire from many of the markets of the world by competitive means at least as "fair" as the means Lancashire has always employed, what is there "fair" in Lancashire's present demand for Japan's voluntary self-restriction? Was Lancashire's old rugged individualism a fair-weather policy only—to be preached when you are winning and to be dropped when you are being defeated? Having derived all the possible advantages from having been the first workshop of the world, do our manufacturers propose to try to retain that accidental supremacy even at the humiliation of begging for it? The question, however, is not one of sentiment, but of fact; and we may be quite certain, therefore, that considerations of force more than of reason will enter into the discussion.   IV 20

It is obvious that if any nation is prepared to subsidize its exports by selling abroad below cost and making up the difference to the home producer by a draft on the National Credit (not necessarily entered anywhere as part of the National Debt)—there is no limit to the variety of Goods it can export and no possible "fair" competition with it by other nations. A nation adopting such a policy can have all the foreign trade it is willing to pay for. Up to the limit of its productive resources and the willingness of its people to foot the bill the trade of the world is completely at its disposal. The only possible means of competing with it is for other exporting nations to adopt the same policy—if they are so minded.

It will be seen, by those who will take the trouble to think about it, that what is implied in this policy is a kind of perverse understanding of the Douglas Credit Theory. The essence of the Douglas proposals consists of (a) the recognition and creation of a National Credit Account—that is to say, of a Monetary facsimile of the total National Wealth both fixed and dynamic; (b) the regulation of retail prices by a ratio of total Production to total Consumption that would allow all consumable Goods to be sold below total Cost; and (c) the institution of National Dividends permitting every individual to participate in the total annual net Production. The subsidies for export under discussion do, therefore, in a veiled way, recognize two, at any rate, of these principles. Being payable not by debt-creation but by the

N

simple means of printing State money for the purpose, the subsidies implicitly if not explicitly assume the existence and availability of a National Credit Account. And being, again, an aid to prices in the form of enabling Goods to be sold below Cost, they embody, likewise, the second of the two main Douglas principles. What, however, is to be noted is that the beneficiaries of this application of Douglasism would be, not the proper recipients of the bounty, namely, the domestic consumers, but foreign nations. It has been suggested that such a policy of subsidizing exports would explain the extraordinary success of Japan's economic, as distinguished from her political Imperialism.   III 19

THE DOMINIONS AND AMERICA

We have no hesitation in saying that the greatest disruptive force of the Empire at this moment is not Japanese competition, or, still less, any centrifugal disposition in the members of the Commonwealth themselves; but, exactly as was the case of the Roman Empire, whose end was foreshadowed in the concentration in Rome of bonds of indebtedness on nine-tenths of the Budgets of all its provinces, it is the Money-Monopoly concentrated in London City. Once mainly domestic only, it is now Imperial, and its bailiffs are in in every Dominion.   IV 20

Newfoundland

A region exists by name Newfoundland and inhabited by a British population of about a quarter of a million, chiefly engaged in fishing. Comes, as Hollywood says, the financier from London. Promising these poor anglers (for whale and cod) riches for nothing—unaware of Mr. McDonald's disapproval—the financier persuades them to borrow money for his exploitation of their resources. They borrow it and incur a debt. In good seasons they manage to keep up their payments, but, after a few bad seasons, helped by the manipulations of the foreign exchange operated by the same financier, they are forced to declare themselves bankrupt. Even, however, with a public and mostly foreign debt, averaging 400 dollars per head (to say nothing of their private debts) the fishers of Newfoundland still form a Dominion; their creditors, that is to say, cannot in their own person take possession and sell the assets to the highest bidder. The creditors therefore have to go to the parent company, England to wit, and persuade her to take over their bonds and to guarantee their security. England in turn for her own security (that is to say, solvency with the same Financier) thereupon does what the Financier may not, and puts the whole estate into a receivership under a Commission. Taking pennies out of a blind man's tin is an amiable peccadillo in comparison with the sordidness of most foreign investment. But in the case of Newfoundland the whole performance is lowered several depths by the certain knowledge of the creditors that their victims were getting over their necks in debts, and by their confidence, justified in the result, that nevertheless when the smash came, the British taxpayer would guarantee their bonds.

IV 7

The Labour members have at last made a stand in the House of Commons and have actually had the temerity to keep the Government up all night on the subject of New-foundland. It is strange that, with all our professed zealots for the Empire, it was left to Mr. Maxton, who pretends to care nothing for it, to defend the sovereign right of a Dominion to go into bankruptcy without having to sur-render its sovereignty to the bailiffs of its creditors. The plans laid down by the financial authorities both for our own parliament and for the superseded government of the late Dominion of Newfoundland were, of course, not affected by the debate in the House; nor was any light thrown, of course, on the identity of the chief villains of the piece. Villains, however, there must undoubtedly have been to account for the state of affairs the Commission discovered in Newfoundland. A population, half the size of Leeds, with only two or three precarious industries as their real credit, could not have contracted a debt of £19 million without the blackguardly connivance and probably at the instigation of "gentlemen" of the City. It is useless to look for their names among the present holders of Newfoundland bonds; but it is a pity that when Lord Amulree's Commission were inquiring into the corruption of the natives they did not take the trouble to inquire who the foreign parties were that traded upon it.   IV 10

The Commonwealth

Separated, it is true, by vast distances and sprawled all over the globe, the component parts of the United States of the British Commonwealth would nevertheless, by virtue of a common sovereignty, a common currency and common trade-agreements, reproduce in effect the organization of the American Commonwealth. The "Empire" would have fulfilled the "wildest dreams" of its present builders, being free-trade within its own boundaries and protectionist towards the rest of the world exactly as the United States of America is today. To realize, however, precisely the value of that ideal consummation, the rainbow-end of the Imperial vision, we have only to look at its actual prototype. If the pattern of a British Commonwealth had already proved to be a glorious success in the case of the American Commonwealth, a very good reason for proceeding with it might perhaps be offered. But with the spectacle before our eyes of the complete and utter failure of such a model of Commonwealth to achieve the solution of a single one of the major economic problems of the world, it is little less than plain idiocy to imagine that a British Commonwealth, modelled on the same pattern, will achieve anything better. In some respects, indeed, the results are bound to be worse. By monopolizing and rationalizing the trade of the Empire, it is certain that all-over Consumption will diminish at a greater rate than all-over Productivity will increase. This, indeed, is the whole object of financial-producer control. And the final outcome of this progressive disproportion of Production and Consumption will be the raising to a grandiose Imperial scale of precisely the same phenomenon that every component nation of the Commonwealth now exhibits. The simple explanation for those capable of understanding anything of economics is this: *If the purchasing-power distributed in each nation of the Commonwealth is insufficient to buy its own total production, the purchasing-power distributed in the whole Commonwealth will be insufficient to buy the total production of the Commonwealth.*   I 7

America

There is no escape for America, or for any other industrialized country with the same problem, by way of a World Conference, even if such Conference should result in a complete agreement on an international medium of exchange. You do not get rid of a problem by simply enlarging its scale. If the disproportion between Production and Purchasing-power within the credit-area of America (or any other industrial nation) results from specific defects in the domestic monetary system, no aggregation of such credit-areas, even though they should amount to the whole world, will have the smallest real effect on any given domestic situation. Under the existing Monetary system, in which all depreciation is debited to Prices and all appreciation is credited to Reserve, every credit-area, small or large, is bound to exhibit the same phenomena. That is to say, a progressive diminution of purchasing-power simultaneous with a progressive increase in collective Overheads, is

certain, sooner or later, to produce, on any scale, the phenomena of "Over-production" and "Under-consumption",
Plenty and Scarcity. Let us suppose, for example, that a
Conference should succeed in making a single credit-area
of the whole of the British Empire, or that a sterling credit-
area should be formed or that the whole world should be
organized as a single credit-area, precisely the same phenomena, only on a bigger scale, will develop in the larger
as in the smaller area. This is one of the strongest arguments
for economic nationalism as an indispensable preliminary
not only to national reform but to world reform. For the
association of nations, each sick of the same internal disease,
is not likely to make a sound international society. Only
when each nation has learned how wisely to use money
within its own credit-area can any good come of attempting
to create still wider credit-areas.   I 8

It does not need any earth-shaking genius to prove that
Credits issued to Producers have the effect simply of raising
Costs and therefore Prices, and hence that without some
compensating financial mechanism for increasing purchasing-power at the same rate that producing-power is increased, the existing top-heaviness of the industrial costing
system is only intensified. Without the creation and free
domestic distribution of purchasing-power equivalent to
the surplus of Production over Consumption it is not only
certain that the condition of America will not improve, but
it is certain that from worse it will go to the worst conceivable. Let nobody on that or this side of the Atlantic lull
himself into the belief that America or this country is getting
out of the wood. We are only beginning to get into it. The
confession which the American railways have had to make,
for example, completely discounts the reports of the menda-

cious Press of both countries of "a more favourable outlook". The Railways, employing a million and a half men, and contributing three hundred million dollars a year to the Budget, complain of the "staggering" deficits they sustained over the three years 1929-32 and of the "complete blackness" of the outlook. In their desperation they invited a Committee of Five that included ex-President Coolidge, Mr. Baruch and ex-Governor Smith, to analyse their financial condition and to "make recommendations". But what recommendations could such a Committee make, that would not involve Federal aid, wage reductions, economy cuts and increased charges for transport—every one of which "sound business" devices is only calculated to reduce still further the purchasing demand available for the use of the railways? The mentality of the type of the persons named is incapable of even looking at the problem from a fresh point of view.   I 25

It is obvious almost to the donkey in the street that the only thing that is short in America is money in people's pockets. And it is equally obvious that the complete control of American money is exercised in the last resort not by the American Government for the American people but by the private financiers who operate the Federal Reserve Bank for themselves and their friends. Putting these two facts together it should then be obvious that the sole cause of the staggering paradox is the divorce between the administration and operation of the collective resources, and their effective monetary control. Without the presence of a single financial racketeer, the people of the United States could administer and operate their resources to their own unparalleled advantage; but being as they are, bound hand and foot by the financial monopoly, they not only cannot operate their plant for themselves, but in a very little while they will have lost more than nominal possession of it. Nine of the largest American railways are (January 1933) already in the hands of the receivers. The City of New York is bankrupt, and therefore completely under the government of private banks. And since the Federal Government itself is unable to "balance its Budget" according to the rules laid down by the banks, the whole of America is practically in receivership. Our forecast that America is headed straight for a ruthless dictatorship is therefore not an item from Old Moore's. The outcome is indicated in the facts of the situation. If the American people owed as much money to a foreign nation as they now owe to their own banks, there would be no doubt about the threatened dictatorship of their foreign creditors. But since their creditors are among themselves, the threat is concealed and consequently its execution is the more easy. II 13

By the grace of God, every other explanation for the plight of America than the simple explanation of a shortage of Money in the pockets of consumers can be ruled out. America is more nearly self-sufficient than any other country in the world. The United States could survive if the rest of the world were to founder. America has all the advantages of Protection and Free Trade simultaneously, being Protectionist abroad and Free-trade in its own continental area. America has a people both industrious and inventive. America has no reparation problem, in the European sense, no foreign indebtedness, no foreign obligations in respect of immediate neighbours. In comparison with our own or any European country, America is free to manage her own domestic affairs without even a thought of her neighbours. In respect of her industrial resources there is no question that they are equal to almost any demand. There is scarcely any nameable commodity, made or grown, of which America has not the actual means of producing enough and to spare not for herself alone but for the whole world. And as for the raw material out of which Money is made, according to the rules of the game, America, as is well known, owns half of the world's total supply. In face of all this, it is trifling or worse to pretend that America's plight is due to anything else than a tragically inadequate *distribution* of purchasing-power. The fact is that the only scarcity in America, as elsewhere, is the scarcity of Money, and this, again, not because the raw material of Money, namely, Gold according to the present system, or Productive Ability according to a sane system, is wanting, but because it suits the greed of the Money-manufacturers to keep their commodity in short supply and the whole nation under constant threat of strangulation.   I 3

America, obviously, has almost infinite resources of labour, plant and raw material—enough, if worked to capacity, to supply almost the whole world and herself as well. The only thing lacking to set the whole of this unparalleled machine in motion is simply money, printed bits of paper, for the most part, when it is not merely figures in a book. What is to prevent America from printing money and distributing it as and how it is calculated to do the most good? The answer will be that this would be inflation. But to this we reply that the present "borrowing" of money from the Banks is also inflation; every bank-loan, large or small, is pure inflation at the expense of the general consumer. And, in the second place, it would be easy to prevent the usual effect of inflation, namely, a rise in prices, by the simple expedient of regulating prices, not by the present idiotic practice of leaving them exposed to the ebb and flow of bank-credits, but by a ratio between Goods actually produced and Goods actually consumed.   I 6

Not only are there no economic forces now at work in America to avert a crisis, but, as far as we can see, there are no positive plans for dealing with it when it is precipitated other than crude force alone. In our own country, similarly headed for catastrophe, we have at least the satisfaction of knowing that there is another string to our bow. A considerable number of influential people among us are fully convinced that, if the worse comes to the worst, as they would put it, there is always the policy of National Dividends to fall back upon. But the principles of Social Credit are too little known in America to be available for use at short notice; and both America's statesmen and their advisers are too conservative and, let us say, too stupid, to be able to grasp them merely on the spur of necessity. Not only, therefore, is it probable that the virtual dictatorship will come into being, but it is equally probable that there will be no happy end to it. The Monetary Monopolists of America are now in complete control of the nation and so long as its statesmen and thinkers are prepared to accept the voice of Wall Street as the voice of God they must endure the penalties of a stringent, ignorant and heartless receivership. It is a spectacle, the humane world will allow, of the very paradox of tragedy. The most enterprising, inventive and hard-working nation the earth has ever known, with resources within its absolute control capable of enabling its people to live like a race of Emperors, with no enemies, actual or potential, to cause it the least fear—compelled, as if by fate, but, in fact, by the stupidity of the many and the cupidity of the few, to suffer as if the nation were an Asiatic horde of barbarians smitten with pestilence and famine. A dozen men in the key positions of American Government who had mastered the not very recondite principles of financial democracy could in a very few weeks create the new order of Society out of the break-up and chaos of the old. But, alas, where are the dozen? Where is one?   II 18

GOVERNMENT

The Bank of England

Ever since 1694, when by an act of royal folly the Crown surrendered to a private corporation the sovereign monopoly of manufacturing money, the House of Commons and the whole machinery of Government have fallen progressively under the control of the Banking monopoly, with the consequence that today, though theoretically the House of Commons has the power of the nation's purse, in practice it would not live a day if it exercised it against the Bank. There is not the smallest sign that the Government or the House of Commons, even if they should realize their responsibility, have the actual as distinct from the constitutional power to exercise it over the heads of the Money Monopoly.   I 3

To the degree of his intelligence, every Chancellor of the Exchequer has realized, on taking office, that in fact the Treasury has no power of the purse any more than the House of Commons itself; and to the degree of his courage and public spirit has been revolted by his discovery. It is not so much the case merely that the advice of the penguins of the "City" has invariably been wrong. From their own point of view, and to judge simply by their present power—our readers must surely be aware that the Banks are now the beneficiary sleeping partners of a considerable part of the total industry of the country—their advice, we should say, has, on the contrary, been invariably right—for themselves.

The anomaly of the situation lies in the fact that, right or wrong, a private institution like the Bank of England is empowered not only to offer advice to the Government but to ensure that its advice is taken.　　　　　I 24

We shall go to our graves staggered, we fear, at the un-awareness of the vast majority of even our educated classes of the nature of the government under which this country lives. Since William II sold the sovereignty of the realm, in respect of the sovereign power of Finance, to the Bank afterwards of England, there has, in fact, been practically no other sovereignty than that of the Bank of England. Commons, Lords and even the Crown itself are little if any more than its political deputies. There is no political party that dares to stand up to it. There is no Parliament that can continue to exist save upon its sufferance. Since the fatal date of 1694 it is safe to say that not only has no legisla-tion been passed and put into effect in this country without the consent and often at the instigation of the Bank of Eng-land, but that no legislation even remotely affecting the interests of the Bank of England has been allowed to be publicly canvassed save within the smallest possible limits and at the maximum disadvantage. It is taken for granted, by an equally astonishing acquiescence in mysterious authority, that the Bank of England is not only beyond public criticism, but under no obligation to define its policy, justify its management of the public credit, or even to publish the names and holdings and interests of its stockholders. So far as any member of the public can possibly know, the ultimate stockholders of the Bank of England may be aliens with interests totally opposed to the interests of the people of England; or they may be people engaged in manipulating the national credit for use against our own manufacturers; or they may be a parcel of nincompoops whom a smart Governor can twist round his finger for the gratification of his lust for power. It is also true that they may be supermen in concealment and patriots slaving for England's prosperity in self-effacing anonymity. On the visible results of their policy, however, there is material for judgment; and, in respect of these, it is a poor consolation to find that only in comparison with the most unfortunate of nations can the English people, the best and most talented people on earth, be said to be fortunate. III 24

It is certainly not the case that Credit Reformers, however much they object to the policy of Banks, including the B.I.S., are under any delusion that banks are unnecessary or that bankers, in this country at least, are not admirable administrators whom it would be difficult to replace. In a Social Credit State, in fact, everything but their present private monopoly of the *use* of the National Credit would be left to them. All that is necessary is that they should become in fact exactly what they claim to be but now are not— the administrators of the National Credit under the direction of a truly national policy. The present old bottles of the financial system can never be filled with new wine. The best to be hoped for from those quarters is the rise of younger men capable of realizing the needs of the age and of adapting banking institutions to them. IV 9

A Nation of poor fish deserves no better Government than a City of sharks. III 17

The Treasury
There can be no dispute that in a democratic constitution such as our own, ultimate sovereignty resides at

least potentially in Parliament and hence that the real villain of the piece is Parliament and, in detail, its financial agent, the National Treasury. It will surely be a matter for astonishment to future ages, when happily the monetary and economic systems of civilized nations will be in automatic harmony, that during several whole generations a sovereign democratic people should not only submit to incredible sufferings, but to sufferings for which the remedy has always been in their own hands. It is perfectly true that the Bank of England is the sovereign by charter of the economic system of this country and thus as immediately responsible for our national condition as, say, the earlier Viceroys were for the conditions of India. It is also and naturally the fact that the Bank of England, like most institutions entrusted with sovereign power (with the exception, it seems, of a democratic Parliament!) should employ every possible means of preserving and increasing its tenure of office and all its privileges. But entrenched and fortified as the Bank of England's position is, the actual fact of the matter is that its Charter is subject to a year's notice of revocation by Parliament, depends for its validity upon the continued consent of Parliament and, in the end, upon the action of the nation's paid Treasury, thus leaving Parliament and the Treasury, and not itself, ultimately and eventually responsible for the conduct of the nation's economic affairs. In all the current discussions of the Monetary system in relation to the collapse of national industry, the Treasury, our paid national office of experts, appears to have completely escaped criticism. The Bank of England is criticized and the politicians are criticized; but nobody ever thinks, it seems, of turning the searchlights of inquiry upon the mysterious but actually all-powerful personnel of the National administration of the national Credit. Between the Bank of England and the

Ministry they have hitherto been effectually screened. It is time that they were brought to book, if not to bell and candle as well.   I 20

Parliament

Everybody knows now that the Government is the rubber-stamp of the Treasury and that the Treasury is the rubber-stamp of the Bank of England.   I 17

Do Members of Parliament, we wonder, realize the depth to which they have sunk in public esteem? Could they conceivably parade and strut knowing nothing and saying nothing as they do if they did? If the nation were at grips with a visible enemy and the Members of Parliament could go to the front now and then on a jaunt of inspection, presumably they would be moved enough occasionally to make the exertion of at least trying to do something about it. But with a far more deadly because more insidious war on, with silent casualties at the vast majority of firesides, our Neanderthals sit around the roast, if not cracking thighbones, cracking jokes. It would appear, moreover, that most of them must be either illiterate or acephalous: illiterate if they cannot read the repeated and demonstrated statements that "Unemployment is incurable as a disease and only susceptible to treatment as a normal and desirable symptom of industrial health", and acephalous if they cannot understand the implication of the statement.   II 11

It is astonishing what camels public opinion will swallow while straining at gnats. A trivial threat to Parliamentary sovereignty such as may be involved in a Tariff agreement of more than five years' duration is debated in Parliament a whole precious week as if the fate of the nation might hang

o

on it. But a slap in the face followed by a kick in the pants from its creature the Central Bank sets any sovereign parliament, Dominion, English or American, bustling to obey even at the cost of the illimitable misery of its own unhappy charges. Quite obviously it is demonstrated that the effective sovereignty of a State is in its currency, and hence that whoever controls the means of payment within a State exercises sovereignty by whatever name it may be called.

II 2

It is a hundred years ago almost to the day when the great Reform Bill was finally passed that placed the responsibility of their economic condition on the people of England themselves. Time has shown that a political democracy without control of its financial system is a democracy only in name. The tiny oligarchy representing the monopoly of Money manufacture has proved itself perfectly capable of effectively governing the country in spite of all the machinery of nominal popular self-government. But what was it that made the country "ripe" for Reform in 1832, and that presumably would indicate its ripeness today? But is the world to wait until its sufferings become so intolerable that the persons of our statesmen are not safe in the streets? Is there never to be a national reform save after prolonged misery and agitation and then only under duress? I 11

It is taken for granted in America—though of course not in our own lily-white country—that a member of parliament represents himself first, the biggest racket in his constituency second, and the interests of the State in his weekends. V 17

The evidence is cumulative, for those who dare to examine

it, that the House of Commons, in spite of all its pretensions
to independence, is, by function, the political "cover" of
the secret gangsters of the Money Racket. So long as by
the usual means, alternately of blackmail and sharing the
plunder, the City's parliamentary accomplices, conscious
and unconscious, can be persuaded not to blow the gaff on
the game, so long can Parliament be indulged in its harmless profession of democracy, free speech and personal
liberty. But let any of its members so much as venture to
call public attention to the real relation of the Bank of England to the Treasury and of both to the City, and their
number is up with the certainty of highly efficient fate.
While this fact is quite well known to the majority of the
members of the House of Commons, it is still a matter of
doubt to a naïve minority; and to the public outside, of
course, it is too shocking to be entertained even as a possibility.   V 9

A National Government, with no enemy or even possible
rival in the land, might have been expected to act in the
interests of the nation at large and within a year at least to
have had something to point to for its stewardship. Musse-
lini, as even *The Times* admits, has during his dictatorship
not only made of Italy "a Guild State" (O shades of our
past!), but he has established a "condition of the people"
that entitles him to rank as "one of the great constructive
statesmen of history". With infinitely greater advantages
and resources, our National Government has failed completely even to touch the problems which the plain citizen
entrusted to it. Foreign trade has been reduced to spasmodic
drippings; the sabotage, by disuse, rationalization and bankruptcy, of our productive plants is continuing unabatedly;
and almost every month a new class of formerly prosperous

citizens is being pressed into the slough of poverty and economic anxiety.   II 2

Ages to come will have something to psycho-analyse in the "case" of a body of public representatives acting, as they claim, under "stern necessity"—in technical jargon a compulsion complex—to reduce the effective money demand on an excessive productive system in the interests of the Bankers' printing-press. It is useless, of course, to invite plain answers to plain questions from these "cases" in their habitual state. But on the chance that moments of common intelligence break the monotony of imbecility even in Members of Parliament, we could wish that these questions should be awaiting them: (1) In what, besides Money, is it a stern necessity that the nation should economize? (Name any Goods or Services of which there is not a practically unlimited national supply.) (2) What or who is it that makes it a stern necessity to keep Money in short supply while everything else is in superabundance? (3) Assuming that you succeed in still further reducing the present paralysingly inadequate monetary demand for Goods and Services, what effect will it be likely to have on the health of "Trade", that is, the sales of Goods and Services? Finally, the question should be put even in this brief examination: (4) How do you distinguish yourselves from moneylenders' bullies, masquerading as the people's guardians?   II 6

Until, in fact, a group arises, inside or outside of Parliament, with brains enough to realize that the problem of Civilization is a Monetary problem, and guts enough to tackle it technically, no Government can be counted on to do any good or even very much more harm. Everything else than the specific is irrelevant; and meanwhile the disease takes its course. I 24

Economics, in the most general sense, applies to the whole system of Production of Goods and Services. We can visualize it as the community in the role of the producer. But Politics, in the same general sense, is concerned not only with the community as producer but with the community as the fulfilment of the needs and hopes of the whole man. There can be no doubt that in the ultimate sense the political aim of every organized society must be to provide for each of its members the conditions favourable to their individual development. And even if, owing to the curse of Adam, communities have hitherto been constrained to subordinate the individual in the interest of the group, the original *raison d'être* of society imperatively demands that the individual shall be freed at the earliest possible moment. Now it is undeniable that every modern community has at this moment the means at its disposal to provide both a progressive abundance of goods and a progressive abundance of leisure to an increasing number of its citizens. And the question of the politics or communal policy involved is reduced to this: has the community in its political capacity the will and the intelligence to utilize its economic resources for the instrumentation of the very purpose for which societies were formed? There are groups and individuals within every society who, strictly speaking, remain prehistoric in their outlook. Still shivering with apprehension of scarcity or, again, still lusting for egoistic power over others, they are perfectly content to see the economic system, long after the need has passed, employed as an agency of government under compulsion. If these conservative elements in society prevail, the course of history for the next few generations is clearly predictable. Individual rights in communal creations and possessions cannot be denied indefinitely with impunity. Sooner or later the individual will break loose, and the resulting forms of society will fall into two types, the Bolshevist and the Fascist, arising respectively from the triumph of the employed or the triumph of the employing classes. In both forms of society, individual liberty will necessarily tend to a minimum as the power of those who exercise State functions tends towards a maximum; and in each instance the victory of the machine over the spirit of Man will once again have been complete. We have reason to believe that Mussolini is not unconscious of all this and, on that very account, is by no means a propagandist of Fascism outside Italy. As between Bolshevism and Fascism he naturally prefers Fascism; but there is, he is aware, a third solution awaiting the advent of a truly modern states-man.   I 12

A National Guild Council, charged with the supervision of specific national productive functions responsibly to the political direction of the State—and having, in consequence, no control as producers but only as citizens, over the *political* question of the wise and proper distribution of the product —is one thing. We who claim to have taught Mussolini much that he knows and much that he has forgotten of the theory of National Guilds have never failed to insist upon the subordination of the economic to the political function. But a State Guild Council charged with both economic and political powers and duties is not only a monstrosity in theory, but in practice it must result in a dictatorship of "big bosses", in comparison with which the "dictatorship of the proletariat" or the oligarchy of Big Business in America would be comparatively Utopian. We do not

believe, of course, that the present craze for Planned Production will be carried to Latin logic in our own country.
But the drift in that direction is unmistakable; and only the
concerted effort of those who realize that the problem of
Democracy is one with the problem of Consumption can
conceivably oppose it effectively.   IV 15

Apart from the political implications of the present drive
towards Planning—the complete surrender of individual
rights to an oligarchy being their logical culmination—
the policy of Planning appears to us to have the following
characteristics among others: It is obviously directed to a
problem that just as obviously no longer exists as such—
the problem of Production which "private enterprise" has
solved many times over. It can therefore be said to be the
Bankers' alternative to any attempt to deal with the only
real economic problem left to society, namely, the problem
of Consumption.

Relatively to Production, Planning can have one of two
possible effects: to increase Production at the cost of increasing Unemployment, both of Labour and of Existing
Capital; or to diminish Production, at the expense of a
rising cost of living. The consequences of the first would be
to intensify the problem of Unemployment and Taxation;
and, of the second, to ensure another era of industrial unrest
in the effort to keep Wages up to Prices.

Even should everything else go according to plan, and
the nation be finally organized in a series of comprehensive
State "Guilds"—the ideal, apparently, of Italian Fascism—
the situation is only made worse. For in addition to the fact
that the State Corporations would be the effective State
itself and capable as such of exercising complete dictatorship,
there would be bound to be created, within the Corporation

of Corporations, degrees of power and authority depending upon economic pulls which no external authority would be in a position to adjudicate upon. As the Electrical Industry, for example, is well aware, if the industries of the community are allowed to become organized under State auspices and in State partnership in defence of their privileges as Producers against the rights of all citizens as Consumers, not only will the Federation of British State Guilds very soon kick the political State downstairs, but within the Federation itself the "Great Powers"—Electricity being the greatest—will very quickly rule all the rest.   IV 14

The Necessary Direction for Future Policy

Force and inertia, the two extremes visible in current politics, are alike products of the despair of reason: the young take to force and the old resign themselves to inertia. And in the continued absence of any evidence in the policy of the Government of the recognition of reason (call it constructive idealism, if you will) it is as good as certain that the mere mechanical swing of the pendulum will defeat the National Government even if it does not bring the "Labour" party into actual and effective power.

Between gratitude for past favours—always a weak motive in politics—and a frustrated future without appeal, it is certain that the "National Government" will fail to renew its mandate, leaving the field to be disputed between the mechanical majority of the "Labour" party on the one side, and the despairing minorities of Fascism and Communism on the other.

If it is useless merely to repeat the dose of the present prescription, it is no less useless, even if it were politically possible, to compound a prescription from the Fascist and Communist formulas. What is necessary is a prescription or rather a regimen that at the same time that it is not immediately revolutionary, like Fascism or Communism, can be counted upon to produce revolutionary changes little by little: a revolutionary idea, in short, rather than a revolutionary act. On the assumptions now or soon to be common property: that the deficiency of Purchasing-power revealed in the widening gap between Scarcity and Abundance, or Consumption and Production, must be deliberately and scientifically made up by the *ad hoc* creation of supplementary Purchasing-power; that Employment in the old sense is and must continue to be an agency of diminishing effectiveness in the distribution of spending-power; that the conditions that have forced Foreign Investment out of existence and introduced Economic Nationalism as the new feature of world economy are likely to continue; and, finally, that only the element of Money is wanting to the full use of the present unlimited productive resources of society—on these now almost unquestioned assumptions, it is certainly possible to lay down a programme answering the requirements that it shall be immediately applicable, progressively ameliorative in effect, implicitly revolutionary, and calculated to enlist the enthusiastic support of both Conservatives of goodwill and the young idealists of Fascism and Communism. The following may be said to be the bare bones which it would be the task of competent propaganda to make live:

1. The Crown's resumption of the sovereign control of the Nation's Credit. (This would involve, not the nationalization of the Bank of England, but merely the revision of the terms of the Bank's present Charter.)

2. The institution of a National Credit Account, preferably drawn up and maintained by a public body such as the Royal Statistical Society. On the Credit side would figure

our Productive assets and their periodical appreciation; and on the Debit side our current Consumption, wastage, loss, and depreciation.

3. With this National Credit Account as the statistical basis for the issue of Money, our Monetary system could thereafter become the increasingly exact reflection, in terms of Money, of the actual facts of our economic situation, Plenty in the real world being represented by Plenty in the Money-world, and real Scarcity by Monetary scarcity —that is to say, by low or high retail prices respectively.

4. The institution, for this purpose, of a retail Price discount system, the discount varying with the state of affairs as shown in the periodical National Credit Account.

5. The gradual introduction of a system of National Dividends (a) in recognition of the principles of the Common Inheritance, and the unearned increment due to continued National association; and (b) as the practical means of encouraging technological development without incurring the horrors of present-day Unemployment.

6. The gradual transfer of all taxation for State services from individual incomes "earned" or "unearned", to the National Credit Account.

If these or anything like them are under discussion as possible planks in a new programme for a National Government, there is certainly hope in constitutional politics. We venture to say that on a programme having these ends in view, not only a National Government, but Parliamentary institutions, and the nation itself, could be saved for both real democracy and real aristocracy.

Very few people are aware of the distance we have already gone in the direction of distributing Goods free or of selling them below cost. At the same moment that all the economic experts are denying that a deficiency of purchasing-power

is necessarily created by the existing system, all the forces
of parliament and public and private charity are being
mobilized to make up the deficiency that is said not to exist
by means of subsidies, grants in aid, bounties, endowments,
doles, outdoor relief and a thousand and one other devices
for concealing the patent fact. There are no statistics available, to our knowledge, to indicate by what exact amount
the gap between total Wages and total Prices is more or less
actually bridged; but, on a rough estimate, we believe that,
as a single item, something like a thousand million pounds
per annum is devoted, by public bodies and private persons,
to no better object than attempting to patch a rent that, in
fact, needs new cloth. Unfortunately, moreover, for this
method of concealing a defect by patching it while pre-
tending that it does not exist, the procedure itself involves even greater evils than those it hides. In the first
place, instead of being drawn from the National Credit
Account at the expense of the community collectively
(that is to say, from the unearned increment of association, which, incidentally, Single-taxers should realize is
common to all property-values, and not to Land alone),
it is taken, by law or by charity, from the pockets of individuals who directly contribute to the National Credit: it
is taken from working Peters and "conveyed", as Shake-
speare calls it, to idle Pauls—by sheer Robin Hood robbery;
and thus, in the ultimate, adds nothing to the total spending-
power. And, in the second place, the practice of one of the
principles of Social Credit in this debased form not only has
the effect of concealing from everybody the fact of the
existence of a gap between Prices and Incomes, but it cor-
rupts at their very sources the possibility of right relations
between citizens by creating on the one side, a class of forced
givers and, on the other side, a class of forced receivers,

and thus making pathological monsters of them both. It will be seen that in one of the planks of the proposed programme, it is suggested that the community should in future do precisely what, in a distorted and left-handed way, it does now—subsidize the difference between Cost and Price by a "free discount"—but only after a frank recognition of the existing gap, out of the National Credit Account, and universally instead of by discrimination.   V 11

The Labour Party

Exactly as the Labour Party has persisted against all reason in repeating the lispings of its infancy referring to the Nationalization of the means of Production, Distribution and Exchange—so in relation to the imagined three-fold enemy of Wages—Rent, Interest and Profits—the party is merely now laying stress on the factor of Interest as once it stressed the factors of Rent and Profits. And exactly as it was useless to show the party, arithmetically, that the distribution of Rent and Profits would benefit the wage-earner only microscopically, it will be equally useless to demonstrate that the abolition of interest-payments to individuals and their complete absorption by the State would, apart from the other consequences, relieve the wage-earner only to the extent, at most, of a few pounds a year.

V 4

The contrast of status of the Trades Union and Labour movement before and since the war is patent and, to its early pioneers, heart-breaking. Only the crawling corpse is left of a once lively and promising body. The main reasons for the early and shameful demise of a once great movement, however, are not far to seek. In the first place, contrary to the advice of all its best friends, the Labour movement

insisted upon confining its outlook to the "welfare" of
merely its own class, with the natural result that even its
own class deserted it (as it always will) when a national
issue was raised. In the second place, ever since the days of
Mr. Keir Hardie the movement has invariably failed to
recognize a leader when it saw one, or, rather, has recognized leaders and leading ideas only to suppress them; witness its studied neglect of men who might have redeemed
its origin—Mr. Shaw, Mr. Cunningham Grahame and others,
its contempt for the Guild idea, now corrupted and taken
over by Fascism, and its positively Threadneedle hostility
to the idea of Social Credit. The most decisive cause of its
decline, however, is to be found in the decline in importance of the economic factor it represents, namely, human
labour. So long as the Labour factor remained more or less
on terms of equality with the Machine in industry, its
representatives could be regarded as of equal even if of
declining importance with the representatives of the
Machine, the Capitalists. But as the importance of the
Machine in industry developed, the relative importance
of the Labour factor was bound to decline until, in fact, it
now corresponds to the value of an obsolescent source of
industrial energy. Economic power, however, precedes and
determines political power. The political pull of the factors
in economics is proportionate to their pull in Industry. Since,
as everybody now knows, of the three main factors engaged
today in Industry, Finance is the greatest and Human Labour
the least, it is an easy matter to predict the continued
decline and final collapse of a Party representative of the
latter alone.   III 22

Abroad

Wake up to the fact that Russia is exporting

Russian-made machinery to Turkey and try to realize what that means. Given the raw materials—skill being in excess supply everywhere—there is literally no nation that is not capable of supplying its own needs or most of them without any assistance from ourselves or America. Technical production is nowadays one of the easiest things in the world to master. Far from being a monopoly of the English or Americans, the very Abyssinians, if they took it into their heads, could have a technical industry in a year or two. In these circumstances to think of again competing in the world at the old advantage is Rip Van Winkleism. The "glory" of Foreign Investment at the expense of the people at home is gone never to return.　　　　I5

Russia

What the world is witnessing in Russia today is the effort of a semi-Asiatic civilization to modernize itself in one desperate and heroic leap. From this point of view the Russian experiment, though revolutionary and not constitutional in origin and method, is not very dissimilar from the effort to modernize herself made less than half a century ago by Japan; and all the talk of Communism and Marx is only the "myth" which the Marxian Sorel required for any successful revolution whatever. And the final and historic result of it all will be, as an Italian observer has predicted, not a Communist, nor even a Collectivist State, but a capitalist State with a powerful bourgeoisie composed of the descendants of the most virile members of the present administrative Communist party. Economic reformers in already modern and completely industrialized communities are wrong, we believe, in looking for light and leading in the social laboratory that is Russia today. As well may the chrysalis try to learn from the caterpillar. A modern industrial community, such as England or America, has a unique and historically unprecedented problem of which nobody in Russia as yet dreams. The Russian problem is to make Plenty. Ours is to learn what to do with it.   II 4

The delusion that Russia is now a Communist State because Communism was the cloak under which the new rulers arrived at power is scarcely calculated to last another five years even among the precious dons at Oxford. And it is practically certain that none of the realists behind the scenes at Geneva have now any other notion of Russia than as one of the Great Powers. It is characteristic of Utopian revolutions that after all the protestations of their fanatics they not only try to preserve themselves, when successful, but everything their nation has acquired before by means either foul or fair. We do not see the new Russian rulers hastening to disembarrass the late Tsar's Empire of any of its ill-gotten gains; nor do we see the Russian Government tolerating even the underground opposition that honeycombed the administration of its predecessor. On the contrary, in point of at least possessive if not acquisitive Imperialism, and in point of tolerating no rival near the throne, the present Government of Russia may be said to have all the qualifications, in the highest degree, for a place among its peers. Let us say at once that far from having any objection to this *fait accompli*, we regard it as both the natural and the desirable outcome of a "Communist" revolution. All unconsciously to the little reds who imagine that Marx was a statesman, the "Communist" movement everywhere depends for its strength and success upon the ambition to govern of previously frustrated classes, each of which, according to type, begins by calling itself the proletariat or what not as a means to its own end. In the case of Russia, though it may be true that Stalin at the top, and a few incorrigible Ivan Ivanovitches at the bottom, retain their "Communist" convictions, the effective Government is steadily being more and more exercised by a new bureaucracy in all probability as corrupt as the last. Russia, in short, has become a Great Power again; and, as such, is of no more and no less a danger to the peace of the world than any other Great Power.   V 23

France

It is undoubtedly true that the policy of Deflation and the policy of Inflation are being carried on in France side by side; but the explanation of this apparent paradox is not either the simplicity or the duplicity of the French political Government; it lies in the simple fact that there are two Governments in France, as there are elsewhere, and that one of them, the political Government at the Quai d'Orsay, is completely subordinate to the other, the financial Government, located at the Bank of France. What, in effect, is the function of the political Government is to cover the policy of the financial Government, in the first place by concealing from the nation the fact that the Bank of France is master and pursues its own interests without reference to the welfare of France; and, in the second place, by playing the Good Samaritan for electoral purposes when the victims of the financial policy become vocal or threatening enough. In all simplicity, there is nothing more in the apparent paradox than this; the explanation explains everything. Given a secret super-national group of men empowered to manipulate the currency in their own interests, and, underneath them, a body of politicians nominally representative of the national interests, but actually, most of them, directly or indirectly, in the pay of the superior group, there is nothing mysterious, nothing even puzzling, in the appearance of the political Government's double role. On the one side, it is the Government's paid business to keep the public in the dark while the deflationary operation is proceeding; and, on the other side, it is equally its business to give the patient a whiff of morphia—in the form of Public Works —when he threatens to become obstreperous. By the obligation to satisfy both demands simultaneously, both the Deflation and the Inflation of the French "Government" are entirely explained.   V 14

WORLD GOVERNMENT: THE VISION AND THE REALITY

Unessentials apart, there is an extraordinary resemblance, amounting almost to complete identity, between the policy being pursued by President Roosevelt and all the other centralized Governments, including our own. All alike think and talk only of Planning; all alike think in terms of planning Production exclusively; and all naturally aim, according to circumstances, at the maximum amount of centralized control and the consequent power to override minorities when the latter are not suppressed from the start. It is not essential to our point of view that we should assume the existence of any collusion among the political or even financial heads of the world today. Similar situations evoke similar responses. All that it is necessary to do is to point out that, in fact and without any hypothesis of deliberate intention, each of the nations now engaged in centralizing industry in the State is doing so under the following identical circumstances. Each is faced with an intense domestic situation of insufficient purchasing-power coupled with Unemployment. Each is or thinks itself to be under the necessity to export more than it imports, regardless of whether it is a debtor or a creditor nation. Each is under the almost unquestioned control of a private Money Monopoly disguised as a National Bank whose interest it is to widen the gap between Consumption and Production for the enlargement of its "reserves". And each is under the illusion, fostered by the Money Monopoly, that the only means of distributing purchasing-power is through the agency of Production, that is to say, by the provision of Employment. There is no doubt whatever in our mind that President Roosevelt and all his colleagues in political world-government are honest men in the old-fashioned sense. No suspicion of vulgar corruption can possibly be attached to Roosevelt or Stalin, Mussolini or Hitler, Kemal Pasha or Ramsay Mac-Donald. They are all honourable men. It is only unfortunately and tragically true that in a crisis of economic history they have all failed, are failing and will probably continue to fail, to see the problem steadily and to see it whole: the problem of raising Consumption to the level of Production, and keeping it there, by intelligent, scientific and, above all, direct means. IV 23

Modestly confessing that he has "little or no organizing power" and is "deficient in most of the qualities of a leader of men", Mr. Wells nevertheless puts forward a conception of world government which would require the organizing ability and leadership of a caste of archangels to carry into effect. Apart, however, from the compensatorily megalo-maniac character of the plan itself—which incidentally is surprisingly similar to that of the apocryphal Protocols of the Elders of Zion—the central assumption of Mr. Wells's dream is the denial of the natural fact of nationality. To Mr. Wells and his very considerable following and company, the existence of nations is a deplorable fact of history but not an acceptable fact of nature. Nations are, but hadn't oughter be. Hence the proposed Society, which he calls X, that is to undertake the ordering of the world, must declare itself "in absolute opposition to the continued existence of separate sovereign governments in the world", and, of course, to this end, aim at creating a single centralized world banking organization and a world money. There can be no doubt whatever that Mr. Wells's support of a world-dictatorship is based upon a strong appeal to the cosmopolitan group of financial "Samurai" now intriguing for the world's throne; but if, as we believe in common with ordinary humanity, nationality is as natural a fact as individuality and one of the essential characteristics of the species Man, then not all the efforts of all the would-be dictators of the world will be able to eradicate it or even suspend its action for more than very brief and bloody periods. We are not so chauvinist as to deny the attraction of the idea of a World Society of Nations, even, if it be possible, of a World Commonwealth of Nations. The emergence, hesitating and amorphous as it is, of a British Commonwealth from the shell of a British Empire, is perhaps a shadow of a possible future. But the difference between a world of nations in intelligent and voluntary co-operation and a world of functional groupings subservient to a Super-State composed of self-selected, all-powerful neurotics, is exactly the difference between a harmonious society of free individuals and a society based on slavery and sanctioned by force. Fortunately for the world, however, both individuality and nationality are constants in the essence of the human race. They may both, and they both do, involve troubles of various kinds; but, in the long run, objective progress is conditioned by their acceptance and conscious use.   I 19

A central Bank, such as the Bank of England here or the Federal Reserve Bank in America, by virtue of its monopoly of the manufacture of Financial Credit, exercises a super-sovereignty over the lives of the citizens within its jurisdiction that extends to the minutest monetary transactions between them. It is the literal fact that, except by barter, no exchange of goods and services can take place between subjects of the same credit-area without the permission of and under the conditions laid down by the super-sovereignty of the Financial authority. Extend this authority to a Central World Bank and it will be seen that whole nations now become subjects of a super-sovereign authority, the rigour of whose legislation, strictly in its own interests, will be unmitigated even by the kinship now more or less actual between "national" Banks and their clients. A world-dictatorship exercised by a World Bank in control of every "national" Bank would not be a mere phrase. On the larger scale implied, the status of every "national" Bank would be reduced, relatively to the central World Bank, to that of any one of the English Joint Stock Banks relatively to the Bank of England. The Bank of England, the American Federal Reserve, the Bank of France, and so on, would, in fact, become, relatively to the central World Bank, scarcely more than a branch, a branch of which, needless to say, the national citizens would be less than twigs or even leaves. Is this the picture of the future that America or any other community of people wishes to paint into actuality?

The situation is really simple. No nation today is in such control of its own Money system that its Government can govern without recourse to Moneylenders. Resulting from the fact that Money is also an international as well as a domestic commodity, the Moneylenders are in a position to regulate international no less than national affairs. Nations, or, rather, the Governments of nations, are their clients in exactly the same way that individuals may be. And exactly as the individual borrower becomes the concern of his Moneylender and, in the final phase, his working pawn, so every State tends to become an unlimited liability company, guaranteed by its citizens, with the Moneylenders as the beneficiaries. Calling Moneylenders Central Banks and their association a World Bank does not change their spots.

18

Mr. Montagu Norman is right in regarding himself as a visionary, but it must be added that as a visionary he is one of the most dangerous that ever lived. In his megalomaniac dreams he sees the world controlled by a Central Bank, housed in a fortress proudly claimed to be built to endure for a thousand years, and administered by a system of financial blockhouses placed at strategic centres over the whole surface of the planet. With a world-monopoly directed from London of the financial medium of all economic and political life, the Governor of the Bank of England and his agents could, as he believes, guarantee the peace and, in his own peculiar definition no doubt, the prosperity of the world for ever. But exactly like all such "altruistic" visionaries, Lenin not excepted, Mr. Montagu Norman appears never to have asked himself what are the conditions of the gratification of his megalomania. Perhaps like Napoleon he would ask what a few million lives are in comparison with his ambition, or, like the harmless visionary Nietzsche, claim that a good fight justifies any cause. But the brute facts of the case are, in the first place, that if he is permitted to pursue his policy, this nation is committed to an epoch of world-wars of which the last was only an affair of outposts; and, in the second place, that even if, in the long run, his policy should succeed, it would be only to make a desolation of the world in the name of peace. Mr. Montagu Norman looks with satisfaction on the record of six new Central Banks created within the nine years concluding in 1934 and all affiliated with the Bank of England. But surely he is not such a visionary as to persuade himself that the rest of the going will be just as easy or, in fact, that it will be possible? On the contrary, his war of conquest is only just beginning, and a thousand engagements must be fought before the World Financial Monopoly can hope to succeed where already on superior ground the Roman Catholic Church has failed. Moreover, his success, as we have pointed out, would be as empty as a graveyard wherein, indeed, all the hopes of mankind would lie buried. The world dictatorship of the proletariat, visionary as it is, and certain as it is, where attempted, to provoke its bureaucratic anti-body, has at least the saving grace of reference to the people at large; it professes sincerely to be only a necessary step to an ultimate democracy. But Mr. Montagu Norman's proposed dictatorship of the Financier has not even the merit of hypocrisy, since it pays not even lip-homage to the human and ineradicable ideal of free men in free societies and of voluntary human co-operation. As a Utopia spun on paper, Mr. Montagu Norman's vision might rank with the equally megalomaniac romances of Mr. H. G. Wells—with whom, indeed, he has many affinities. But we have only to imagine Mr. Wells at the Bank of England to realize how dangerous Mr. Montagu Norman is, and the more so from the fact that he appears to be as irresistible to his colleagues as Mr. Wells to his readers.   V 26

Every ambitious or threatened dictatorship has sought the alliance of the genuine idealism of its day, and in the case of the dictatorship of International Finance the ally it has sought and found is that of the League of Nations. A League of Nations co-operating "to outlaw war, to improve social conditions, to preserve individual human rights and to further social justice" must command, on the face of it, the allegiance of the best elements in human society. Only the sub-human in one form or other could possibly be opposed to it. But the League of Nations that was born of the War has only a comparatively weak strain of its idealist progenitor. Its prepotent contributory was the will, not to ensure the nations against future wars, but to assure the victors of the latest their spoils. It was not only a League primarily of victors, but, even more fundamentally, it rapidly assumed the character of an assembly of Debtors and Creditors. Finally, its nurse and foster-parent has been and still is, not the best public opinion of the world, but, as everybody now knows, the expert interested opinion of the delegates of the private Central Banks of the world operating as the Bank of International Settlements. III 6

There is nothing really mysterious or recondite in either the policy or the tactics of Central Banks individually or collectively. It is what Major Douglas calls the "black magic" of the business that obscures from ordinary people the simple operations of simple motives. Ordinary people have been "hypnotized" into believing that the workings of World Finance are a mystery beyond their comprehension and, moreover, that it is something of a blasphemy, liable to punishment, for anybody to question the sacred authority. In the simplest if unfortunately not in the most easily realized terms, however, the truth about the policy and the tactics of the Money Monopolists is this: their policy is to get everybody into their debt as completely and hopelessly as possible; and the means they employ to this end is first to strip their own nationals of purchasing-power and thereafter to lend the loot abroad for the purpose of similarly stripping other nations. We have not the least hope, of course, that the present generation will be able to perceive the literal truth of what we have just said. Protestants of the Establishment of Mammon are as liable to be understood as Protestants of the time of Copernicus or Bruno. But we can point at least to the evidence in confirmation of our description, and challenge anybody to deny that the "Money authorities" in every State do, in fact, steadily and consistently preach and compel the practice of (*a*) economy, that is to say, the restriction of purchasing-power at home; and (*b*) "international trade", that is to say, the lending of as much purchasing-power as possible abroad. It is not just a coincidence that these two objects should be concurrently and simultaneously pursued by the Central Banks. They are the very *raison d'être* of the Monopoly of Money. And we are so far from ascribing any unusual devilry to the individuals unhappily afflicted with the mania for Money-power, that we can sincerely affirm that if angels from heaven were commissioned to establish and maintain a Money-monopoly, they would in all probability proceed on the same lines as the present authorities, though, of course, with rather more intelligence!   III 3

WAR AND PEACE

War

What should they know of England who read only the English Press? All Europe was excited during the third week of January 1934, by the disclosure in an Italian official report that England had started upon another Naval-building race, her particular rivals being the United States and Japan. Without assuming that the report was correct in all its details, it may be taken for granted that its substance was true, since it is the logical sequel to the policy of Foreign Investment in a contracting field. The supposition that Armaments can be limited while nations are engaged, by their Cities, in a life and death struggle is pure illusion; and equally illusory is the belief, entertained by most pacifists, that War is instigated by Armament-makers or by chauvinism. Such a map will never be exhibited in public, but we have little doubt that somewhere or other it exists—that shows the distribution and ownership of the world's foreign investments as well as of its potential supply of fields for investment. And it would be in relation to such a map that the foreign policies of the various leading nations of the world would perhaps begin to become publicly intelligible. The astonishing thing, even in its absence, however, is the ease with which the educated public can be persuaded to believe that the welfare and honour of their nation are at stake when all that is usually in question is a financial debt whose beneficiaries, though having an address in the City, are not even always British by birth or even adoption.

The same educated public opinion was expressed in *The Times* of the same week in connection with the then current war between Bolivia and Paraguay. Not only for the most part did none of the suffering combatants on either side know in the least why they were being slaughtered, but, according to *The Times*, it was a "mystery" how two States in the weakest financial condition could equip themselves with the most costly and modern weapons. But the mystery is not impenetrably profound. Rival bondholders in the Chaco were engaged in one of their minor disputes to which they were prepared to sacrifice merely a couple of small nations. Bondholders on a larger scale and on a wider field are prepared to sacrifice correspondingly greater nations, few of whose members either will have the remotest idea of what it is actually all about.   IV 14

We all know that the English and Australian troops who were blown to bits in the Dardanelles died happier for realizing that the guns that destroyed them were British made; and similarly the phosgene gas that suffocated French troops was the more welcome for having been made of French carbon bisulphide. Dying by as well as for one's country is a double bliss and it appears that our world-dictators are not going to deny it to us.   I 14

The Causes

Armaments do not make war, any more than Disarmament would prevent it. It has to be remembered that both war-talk and war-preparation have their uses in the black art of modern government. Threatened with war, a nation will allow its purchasing-power to be extracted almost to the last stump before kicking out its financial dentists; and, as a popular means of at once creating a

Debt to the Banks and Public Works for Employment, there is nothing, as our members of parliament know, like preparing for war; even the taxpayers suffer gladly.   V 7

Men only murder each other when in pathological conflict. War, in short, is a disease and not one of the normal appetites of man. The real difficulties in the path of progress derive from the simple time-dishonoured fact that every nation not only suffers from the restriction of its own domestic credit, but is compelled, as a consequence of that restriction, to seek relief in foreign markets either as creditor or as debtor. And as with every invention the relative scope of the available world market is constantly diminishing while, at the same time, the necessity of domestic relief is constantly increasing, the struggle for national maintenance, both inside and out, becomes more and more pathological. There is not the smallest possibility in these circumstances that nations will agree to disarm or, even if they formally agree, that their agreements will be kept. Nor could a reconstituted League of Nations, all engaged in internecine economic war, offer the smallest hope of international peace. Both Disarmament and the League of Nations represent efforts to pretend that the disease can be treated by regulating its symptoms; and they both proceed from wilful ignorance of the fact that the disease is too deep-seated for plasters. We affirm, in the spirit of prophecy, that there will be no secure peace on earth and no effective goodwill among nations until every nation recovers its own financial autonomy. There is literally nothing else economically wrong with the world but its financial system.   IV 22

Without completely accepting Marx's theory of the economic determination of history—of which, indeed, the

apocalyptic Ireland is a perpetual contradiction—there is no
need even to prove that the relation between Foreign trade,
for example, and Armaments is infinitely closer than the
relation, let us say, between political ideas and Armaments.
Wars today, as has often been remarked, do not break out
on account of scarcity; nor are they, if they ever were, wars
of wanton conquest. All modern wars, including the last
and the next, are the result of competition for foreign
markets in which, relatively to the competing Supply, the
Demand is contracting. Imagine a number of growing
nations competing not for the means to live but for fields
of investment. As their needs and numbers multiply, so,
too, the struggle for the bottle-neck of a contracting field
intensifies. Be the nations as lambs in their intentions, they
will act like wolves when the pinch comes, if only they
have the strength at command. It is a farce in this situation
to discuss the limitation of armaments, qualitative disarmament, the illegalization of poison-gas and the like. On the
other hand, the real remedy against war, namely, the removal
in every industrial nation of the *need* for foreign investment
—a fancied need excused on the plea of the employment
that exports without imports gives—would necessitate a
revolution in our Monetary-system, and of the alternatives
of such a change and War, the vast majority of people,
whether from apathy, superstition, or dope in one form or
another, prefer, it seems, the easy familiar alternative of
War.   I 3

Most of our Liberal thinkers of today assume that the
causes responsible for the world chaos are ideological rather
than material and hence that the proper treatment of the
condition is ethical rather than economic. To any realistic
observer the fact that, owing to the development and spread

of mechanical production, nations are inevitably becoming increasingly self-sufficient, is explanation enough of the revival of nationalism without seeking other and purely psychological causes. And equally the fact that the era of Foreign Trade in the old sense is definitely over makes it certain that henceforward every nation must learn how to distribute its production at home or undergo the painful experience of crude revolution. Liberalism, on the other hand, is still under the delusion that Foreign Trade is not only indispensable to national prosperity but can and ought to be internationally controlled. Seeing what is the fact, namely, that the great exporting nations are rapidly drifting towards collision and another and greater World War, Liberals conclude that the cause is not what it is, namely, the failure of such nations to consume their own production at home coupled with the natural shrinkage of Foreign Trade, but the wilfulness of nations seeking independence and power, so to say, spontaneously and not under compulsion. Their proposals naturally follow this analysis and it is to be observed that they are identical with the plans of the very Power against which no doubt the Liberal school imagine themselves to be in polar conflict—the Money Monopoly of the world. They advocate, for instance, "a gradual sapping of the idea of national sovereignty", the extension of the mandatory system under the League of Nations, and, above all, "the centralized control of Gold", exactly as if they were in league with International Finance instead of opposed to it. The whole of Liberal thought to-day, indeed, is in our judgment dangerously reactionary from its complete failure to recognize the aims and character of its executive colleague.   I 18

The supposition that "nationality" is a Moloch that

demands blood-sacrifice is plausible in the light of existing
international relations. But, in fact, it is no more sensible
than to attribute wolfish bloodthirstiness to dogs that have
been kept starved and chained in a prairie of plenty. So far
from nations being naturally disposed to war, it takes, as
we know, an enormous amount of "propaganda" to get
their "blood up". And the most effective means, the Central
Banks have discovered, is to keep them all domestically
exploited—that is to say, starved and wretched—and then
to tell them that some other nation is to blame.   I 25

The causes of war are not to be found in political or
economic nationalism, but first of all, in the fact that no
nation is allowed the financial means of buying the whole
of its own Production, and, secondly, in the consequential
fact that the "surplus" must be exported as an "investment"
if it is to be accounted for at all. The first fact produces the
"unrest" that renders the nation an easy victim of armament-
makers, foreign investment-mongers and, incidentally, of
crazy doctrines of Communism and Fascism. And the second
fact produces the international friction that begins as trade-
competition and ends in the flame of war.   IV 4

The fancy that, by agreement not to exercise their rights
of self-preservation, you can ensure that, when threatened,
nations will not go to war with sticks and stones if need be,
is literally inhuman; and equally it is inhuman to pick and
choose among the victims and to declare that this or the
other began it. It reminds us of the ingenious training the
late Charles Peace, of blessed memory, is said to have given
himself before embarking on his public career of murder.
He would tie cats in pairs by their tails, swing them over a
clothes-line, and then have revolver practice with the first

cats to claw the others. We are, of course, not suggesting
that there is anything more than a striking resemblance between the aptly-named Charlie's attempts to preserve inter-
feline law and order, and the attempts of the other Peace
Conferences to regulate teeth and claws and to visit breaches
of the rules with superior force. All that our comparison is
designed to suggest is that while cats in their free state may
be quarrelsome enough, they are pretty certain to be both
murderous and suicidal when death in any case is before them.
We have yet to hear of really prosperous nations going to
war; or of nations threatened with economic extinction failing to go to war or, in the alternative, committing the
suicide of revolution. There is, in fact, no problem of War
as such in modern society; but always it is the secondary
phenomenon of economic conditions that in themselves
tend to become unbearable. Pious old geezers of all ages,
classes and sexes, will do nothing against War even to delay
it by a year. Only the practical solution of the prior problem
of Distribution will put an end to war. This alone is the
spirit of Peace. Pacifism without it is sentimentality.   III 24

If borrowing and lending among individuals oft doth lose
both loan and friend, it is not irrational to suppose that the
cash-nexus between nations tends to distort and warp the
natural feelings of the lenders into a feverish anxiety for the
security of their loans, and of the borrowers into a chronic
resentment at having to repay them. However that may be,
there is not the smallest doubt for any "realist" that in practice the foreign policies of the various governments are at
least powerfully influenced by their international relations
as present and prospective Creditors and Debtors; and sufficiently, for all practical purposes, to enable us both to
"explain" particular policies and to guess the probable

course of large events. Without venturing into prophecy for the moment, we would invite our "pacifist" readers to avert their gaze awhile from the spectacle that now appals both them and us of the prospective resumption of competition in armament building, and to inquire into the relative distribution among the nations most concerned of (*a*) their present foreign loans and investments; and (*b*) their prospective loans and investments. We are not concerned in this inquiry with the conditions, financial and other, indispensable to legitimate foreign trade, that is to say, to the complementary exchange of Goods and Services. No two nations in complementary relation have ever gone to war with each other, we believe; nor ever will. Only creditor and debtor nations make war. The inquiry is confined to the foreign trade in money, to the relations of the "Cities", in short, and not of the peoples. The results, we predict, will startle even pacifists, and perhaps wake them at last to the realities of which armaments and even whole peoples are only the tools.   IV 5

It is probable that not one per cent of the American population were clamouring for war while President Wilson was promising their intervention. But it is also probable that not one per cent were opposed to it, once the order had been given. We implore our pacifists to try to realize that war is an induced madness that no nation may not succumb to. So long as Foreign Trade is regarded as indispensable to national prosperity, and in face of the undeniable certainty that Foreign Trade is declining at the same rate at which Production is increasing—so long will the madness of war be inducible, and at shorter and shorter notice.   I 17

Armament

If the lips now sealed were to speak, it would be revealed that the effective movement towards our national disarmament, like the present effective movement towards rearmament, was and is initiated and put into execution by people whose concern with peace or war is far above or below the plane of sentiment; on the realistic plane, in short, of Finance. Hitherto it has not suited these people to allow our Budget to be unbalanced, as France's Budget is, as Japan's Budget is, and as America's Budget is. Oh, no, we must only defend ourselves within our poor shrunken means. Should the time come, however, when the armament of England becomes necessary to the higher powers, the canons of sound finance will be the first to go off; and all the claque of the economists now applauding economy will be throwing up their caps for unlimited expenditure and damn the consequences.   IV 8

Before entering on an armament race, it is important that our genuine peace-lovers should consider why this calamity may be about to befall us. It is intolerable that they should remain under the delusions that the resumption of Armaments will be due to any nation's spontaneous bellicosity or to the machinations of armament contractors or even to such psychological causes as national pride or national resentment. There is no doubt that the presence of any one or all of these factors in a given situation may contribute to the decision of the question of war; but neither singly nor collectively can they be regarded as the actual causes of war. Quite simply the causes of war are economic; and they begin, like most things, at home. Given the fact—though it is really no assumption but rather an axiom—that the purchasing-power distributed at home is insufficient to buy the total national Production, it becomes obligatory and imperative that the surplus Production (or, if it be preferred, the complementary purchasing-power) be exported. The foreign markets for the absorption of these surpluses, however, tend inevitably to contract, and at approximately the same rate at which the surpluses of the credit-exporting countries tend to expand; with the ironic consequence that almost exactly to the degree that the export of surpluses becomes more and more domestically urgent, the possible foreign market for their absorption becomes less and less receptive. If now to this situation we add the fact that, even apart from the mathematical impossibility of disposing of a constantly increasing surplus of Goods in a constantly contracting market, the principal nations are already over-borrowed or over-lent—involving them, in either case, in an added difficulty—it will be seen that sooner or later one or other of the nations is bound to blow up either internally or externally. Internally if there appears to be no hope of external expansion—from the prospect of a favourable war, for example. And externally, that is to say, by war, if the chances of victory appear to be short of completely desperate. This analysis, we believe, holds good not of one or two nations only, but of all; and its validity is independent of any of the factors previously named.   IV 6

To Procure Peace

As a practical problem offered to nations in earnest about Peace nothing would be easier to bring about than the abolition of war. All you have to do is to make peace so profitable in all senses and to all nations that war would appear to be suicide; and this could be effected by instituting in each nation a Credit system that not only made foreign exploitation unnecessary but ensured for every citizen inalienable dividend-rights in a progressive national enterprise. We are aware that it is "naïve" to suggest that the problem is as simple as this or that it is susceptible of so simple a solution. The clever imbeciles of every nation prefer, like the fools of Scripture, to keep their eyes on the ends of the earth and to fetch a compass before even calling on their neighbour next door. The professed pacifists, no less than the human "warrior ants" (like Hitler and Mussolini, who prescribe war for eugenics and the soul) are at one in this, that sooner than consider the "naïve" proposal to end war by eradicating its causes (all Wars are financial), they will cudgel their poor brains to invent imaginary causes for which they then proceed to concoct and apply imaginary remedies. The resultant of it all is to be seen in the extinction of one of the few remaining hopes of mankind—the faith that Reason will one day prevail. It was admitted in *The Times* (which, however, did not fail to sneer at the *naïveté* of normal men) that the Disarmament Conference presented at its demise "a sad story of high hopes dispelled, of opportunities lost, of concessions made too late, and changes of mind that nullified small advances". Yet we have no doubt that every one of the steps that led to this result was acclaimed as practical, realistic, objective, and all the rest of it, in contradistinction from anything which the scum of mankind could pronounce naïve. The outcome, furthermore, while it may make angels weep, will not be inacceptable to the interests whose wishes have dominated the result. The masses may suffer, having, as Mussolini says, reserves of unimagined asceticism and heroism to reveal in the beautiful blood-stained struggles of glorious war. But, on the other hand, the preservation of the constant menace of war will ensure the survival not only of dictators, but of their janissaries, the armament-makers, and, in addition, will provide them with a Public Works' policy to which neither taxpayer nor "expert" economists will offer the smallest objection. Since everybody but everybody is therefore likely to be self-satisfied, it is a pity that we have to suggest that an Armaments race and a Budget balanced by "sound finance" are not compatible in the long gallop. Whether by Peace, by War, or by Preparation for War, the future is with the unbalanced Budget; the principles of "sound finance" are doomed in any event. V 8

Until genuine pacifists decline to follow the lead of the interested authorities and begin thinking in real terms, their propaganda is not only doomed to fail, but, infinitely worse, to assist the enemy by collusion. It is one of the most tragical facts that among the forces most hostile to the principles of Social Credit are the official Peace groups and parties.

IV 10

We are not trying to be paradoxical beyond the actual facts; but it appears to us to be simply incontrovertible that a nation idiotic enough to pursue a favourable balance of trade *and* the prostitution of Industry to the function of providing Employment, must not only tolerate but support, secretly or openly, an industry like the Armament industry, that implements both policies. Who wills the end wills the means; and though it is true that the means in this case are devilish, it is only because the end in view is devilish. The Armament-makers, in fact, are only doing the dirty work of the Bank of England and all it stands for. V 23

If the hegemony of World-finance instrumented by the lion's share of World-investment is the settled objective of the present rulers of this unhappy country, the sooner the

Army, Navy and Air Force demand a proper equipment for their double task of attacking other countries and defending their own, the sooner will the issue of the People versus the Banks become clear. II 22

It is true that we may be some years off the realization of Mr. Shaw's picture of a party of scientists going off to war with a lunch-basket and an assortment of scientific gadgets. But it is nevertheless true that exactly in proportion as Production in general becomes more efficient, more specialized and in need of fewer and fewer men to operate it, the particular Production of hostile casualties ought to be and can be effected in the same labour-saving manner. We are aware of course, that the objection will be raised that the introduction of more machinery into the industry of war will tend to throw an increasing number of people out of occasional employment; and that from this point of view even the bayonet and the rifle may be defended as a return to handicraft. But as it is probable that not all the War Offices of the world can be simultaneously persuaded to forgo the use of Science in the interests of the simple death, it will go hard with the nation whose War Department insists upon regarding itself as an agency for providing occasional universal employment. If the policy of World-competition for areas of investment is to be continued, with its constant attendant risk of war as the final sanction, there is nothing to be done but to raise the level of the technical efficiency of the forces beyond all probable rivalry. As it is, the nation is accepting a commercial policy that inevitably involves a succession of wars and at the same time a military leadership that must inevitably make each war more suicidal. IV 13

Assuming it to be necessary to the welfare of the nation and hence to the individuals composing it that the nation should at least be able to defend itself, military, naval and air-power are not, it is obvious, the only weapons it must keep bright and ready. The physique and the morale of the nation, and not of the fighting forces alone, are of equal and, indeed, greater importance. And greatest of all, though all unrealized by "mediocre" statesmen, are the things by which the soul of a nation lives—Wordsworth's admiration, hope and love. The now common degeneracy of Englishmen in respect of power has its parallels, if not its actual cause, in degeneracies in other fields—in housing, in education, in food and clothing, and, above all, it has its parallel, if not its cause, in the degeneracy of the functions proper to normal man of admiration for his superiors, hope for himself, and love for his fellows. We may not be—such is the state of the world at large—fifth in rank in respect of these, as we are, say, in air-force; but the sorrowful and bitter truth is that in respect of everything we are fast declining.   II 7

PROPOSALS

We beg readers not to be affected by the charge of Utopianism brought against the proposals advocated in these
pages. It is true that on the respective scales now trembling
in the balance are prospects for Mankind that may be described as Utopian and prospects equally truly describable
as diabolical and hellish. But at the present juncture it is
rather fear for civilization than love of a possible culture that
must animate the most practical minds.   IV 15

The breakdown we are now witnessing of the "Capitalist"
system is due to this simple but cumulative cause—that
hitherto, and still, it is the producer alone who receives
Credit. His are the interests exclusively kept in view by
the Banks and their Government agents, on the demon-
strably false supposition that if only a progressive Production
is secured, a progressive Consumption is bound to follow.
The whole wretched world can see how mistaken it all is to
continue pouring Money into Production and simultaneously draining Consumption of any possible equivalent purchasing-power. And if the world is to escape its present
apparent doom, it is obvious that immediately and henceforward the Credits hitherto issued to Production alone must
be issued to Consumption also. The machinery for effecting
this diversion and division of Credit between the Producer
and the Consumer is perfectly simple. Should it become the
declared Monetary policy of the nation to employ Money
to effect not only the maximum Production of Goods but
their maximum Distribution for Consumption, no World

Conference would be needed to formulate or approve the means. We undertake to say that once this *objective* of national Money policy were clearly adopted, a Commission of Accountancy Experts could draft the enabling legislative measures in a month. The essential and fatal defect of the "Capitalist" system, namely, its inability to instrument Consumption simultaneously and proportionately with Production, would be removed; and our nation, at least, and probably the rest of the world, would be spared the horrors of its impending collapse.   19

In an admirable State-paper drafted by Mr. George Thorpe and ordered to be published by the American Senate, the principles of a sound communal Monetary system are laid down. No metallic base or other arbitrary symbol is necessary for the measurement of the amount of effective demand upon its own production that a nation can be allowed, but the basis of Money is clearly defined as the total resources of the community as a whole—in short, its Real Credit. There is no mincing of the implications either, in the historic document to which we have referred. The monetary unit, dollar or what not, is what the State defines it to be, and there can be no competing or overriding definition. (This in reply to the bankers who protested that President Roosevelt had no constitutional right to dissever their Gold from the nation's Money.) And as for the communal ownership of Real Credit, the proposition is unequivocally affirmed that "the ultimate ownership of all property is the State", private ownership, "so called", being only a matter of social expediency and convenience. It is important to realize as clearly as the authors of this protocol that, in effect, the existence of legal tender is itself, by implication, the admission of complete communal ownership. If the State alone can define and create legal tender, and all such tender becomes a legal and enforceable claim on any property whatever, then it obviously follows that the State's right to create Money presupposes the State's right to the disposition of all property. What we are suffering from today is, in fact, the restriction of this sovereign right and its chartered exercise by a private corporation. There is, of course, no question that by their licence to create Money the Banks do in fact exercise control over all property, thus usurping the sovereignty of the State. And it is not only no mitigation, it is an aggravation of the offence, when the Banks claim that at least they confine the exercise of their sovereignty to a multiple of the metal Gold.   III 11

The problem before Civilization today is not one of the usual ups and downs of the Industrial system. In the absence of a miracle or of a giant consumer in the form of another Great War, it is arithmetically certain that Production relatively to Consumption has now become so top-heavy that, like the Tower of Babel at a certain height, the whole edifice of Industrialism will topple down. There is yet time, in our opinion, for a purposive overhauling and reorientation; but the condition of its efficacy is precisely a common agreement as to our future objective. The more or less obvious drift of things today is in the direction of the objective of the Money Monopolists—that is to say, the Financial dictatorship of the world, with whole nations as victims. And the "planners" and the tariffists, the "stabilizers" and the "inflationists" form no effective opposition to this centralizing of world-control, for the simple reason that they cannot or dare not formulate a counter-objective. We will state it for them in a few words. The proper human objective of a modern Industrial State, we affirm, is the maximum Production and maximum Distribution of the best Goods and Services with the minimum of human labour and the maximum of Leisure for All. Money is an instrumental agency in this. There is everything in the world and society to make this objective as practical as it is, outside abnormal minds, universally desirable. And with something approaching the Promised Land of Science and Invention within sight and reach, it will be another of the tragedies of Mankind if the world is cheated of its realization by a few fanatical worshippers of the Golden Calf.   I 9

Call it capitalist or individualist, private enterprise or exploitation, the fact remains that, in respect of Production and the means of Production, the system as we kown it has surpassed the most extravagant promises of its authors. On the other hand, call it again what you please, Sound Finance, or the immutable principles of Economics, there is obviously no greater failure in the world today than that of the Banking System to deal with the problem of Distribution.

III 21

The order of procedure for escape from the world's present tragical and yet hopeful dilemma is Organization of Consumption first, and Planning for Production only secondly and consequentially. It is preposterous to contend as many do, that the problem of the organization of Consumption is more difficult or more complicated than the problem of the organization of Production. The truth, in fact, is just the reverse, the problem of Consumption in relation to that of Production being parallel with the printing and distribution of, say, railway tickets compared with the construction of a working railway system. A mere fraction of the thought devoted to the problem of Production (and, incidentally, of the friction arising from efforts to organize Production on the unnatural basis of money-considerations), would enable the world to solve the problem of Consumption and to proceed thereafter with a light heart to the solution of the minor problem of Production. It is the criterion of sound intelligence in economics today that the two problems are seen in their proper order of importance, as it is the condition of any progress that they shall be solved in that order. We affirm, indeed, that in no other order is the practical solution of either problem possible.   III 20

The cry that what is needed today is More Production or More Sources of Production is unworthy of a parrot. Only the type of mind of the miser of fiction is capable of demanding more and more of what he has already in excess and is too demented to make use of.

The "cheap money", now in such evidence in the Money Market, is not of the smallest use to an industrial system glutted with Goods for want of customers. Nor, again, if credit were absolutely free would it set the wheels of industry moving again, in the absence of a market composed exclusively of Wages, Salaries and Dividends. The fact is that all our present efforts to revive industry begin at the wrong end, at the end already surfeited with means. The proper end at which to pump in new credit is at the consuming and not the producing end, and this can only be effected by a distribution, throughout the consuming community, of non-repayable credits either in the form of National Dividends or in the form of what is called the Just Price ratio.   I 6

There is literally no means of increasing Consumption relatively to Production other than by creating purchasing-power that precisely has *not* passed through the Productive accounts. And there are, as far as we know, no other means of doing this than the time-honoured means of Dividends; in the case of the nation at large, of National Dividends.

II 17

What is both necessary and practicable—and, in the end, inevitable if society is to survive—is the creation of a National Financial Credit Account that shall represent, in terms of money, the Real Industrial Credit Account of the nation, and be simultaneously debited with the cost of enhancing the nation's wealth and credited with the resultant enhancement. From such a National Fund it would be possible to support practically all the national services, including National Dividends, without recourse to either loans or taxation. Half a dozen competent engineer-economists could in a week or two draft a practical scheme to this effect.   I 26

POLICY AND PROSPECTS OF THE MONEY REFORM MOVEMENT

A radical Monetary reform is possible under two forms of Government only—a dictatorship which, of course, implies a precedent Revolution—or a "Patriotic Government" largely and predominantly composed of "Tory aristocrats", by whatever name they may be called. To expect, for instance, that our own Labour party, supplemented however it may be, by the Liberal party, could, even if it had the will and the nominal power, transform our Monetary system without precipitating defeat or Revolution, is to fly in the face of fact and reason. On the other hand, it is equally certain that unless under the stress of desperate class necessity, the "Tory aristocrats" of all nations will continue in effect indifferent. It remains to be seen whether the national necessity will become desperate enough to invade and imperil the lives of the classes we refer to. The signs are that it will.   I 6

Certainly there is a solid inertia in the British character that makes resistance to tyranny rather a fact than a virtue; but, on the other hand, not only have there been dictatorships in England before, but they have invariably occurred when the forces in opposition have each claimed to be absolute. When absolute Monarchy encountered the claim of absolute Democracy, a dictatorship of either Left or Right was the only possible solution. And similarly if the present Monopoly of Money now concentrated in the Treasury and the Bank of England (completely over the heads, it is plain, not only of Parliament but of the Crown) should decide to make an absolute issue of it, there is nothing in the long run that we can see to challenge it effectively but a dictatorship of some kind, constitutional as in the United States or irregular as in Italy and elsewhere. The question, however, is still to be answered whether, in fact, either the claim will be made in absolute form or, if made, whether it will not evoke an opposition effective without violence. The really influential classes in this country have not yet awakened either to their opportunities or to their peril. Unlike their hero, Drake, who indeed played bowls until the Armada was sighted but had his fleet in readiness for immediate action, the middle classes of England today are playing bowls and leaving their defences unprepared. Almost at any moment the enemy may be down upon us in the form of a dictatorship, and then it will be too late to take sweet counsel together save in the Labour or Concentration camps to which, as will be just, the neglectful custodians of liberty and social betterment will be the first to be despatched. Again the question is chiefly one of time. Can the effectively intelligent classes be awakened before it is too late, and, on their awaking, be made to see that for forms of government only fools and maniacs for power contend, but that for an adult nation it is policy, policy, policy that matters?   V 3

Assume that the monopoly of the incredibly profitable and powerful control of the nation's and, ultimately, of the world's credit has, by the equally incredible folly of society, been given to a group of private individuals; assume that, according to their own rules, the unquestioned maintenance of their privilege depends upon their keeping money for Consumption in short supply while accumulating more and more lavish supplies of money to be lent for Production, by means of the so-called Gold Standard—the details of the administration of such a policy are matters of tactics rather than of strategy. No sovereign power, religious or secular, has ever voluntarily abdicated; and it is contrary to all history either that a sovereign can "plot" to preserve his power or be merely persuaded to surrender it. In the circumstances of the sovereign power of Finance, the natural objective of its representatives is to maintain and, if possible, to extend it—cost what it may to the nation or the world at large or even ultimately to themselves. Sooner or later, if the sovereign system in question proves to be incompatible with human progress, something breaks, either the sovereignty itself or the nation over which it is exercised or both.   I 16

Sooner or later every community that fails to adjust its Consumptive to its Productive system will reach the state in which despair will overwhelm reason and violence will be called in. We are a long way from open violence in our own country, and may its day never come; but of the deadly violence of poverty in all its forms concealed under the cloak of the most proficient hypocrisy the world has ever known, our own country has more than enough.   V 16

In contrast with the experimental constitutions now springing up like fungi in the rank soil of the Depression, there is much to be said for our old parliamentary regime. It is pre-eminently fitted for a race that has only one rule for great men—to slander them in private and to smother them in silence; and it is admirably adapted to the peculiar superstition of Britons that never, never will they be slaves, save of themselves. We can foresee no emergency in which the British will be either imaginative enough to select a leader of genius or intellectually energetic enough to be ashamed of muddling through. And the institution of parliamentary government with its overwhelming preference for mediocrity is exactly the sort of slow motion which the average mind can follow. That behind the screen are the operative bureaucracy and behind them, again, the financial magnates of the great politico-economic film world, the crowds that applaud or criticize the performance scarcely even suspect with the result that we can have all the Fascism or, for the matter of that, all the Communism our magnates like, with the crowds not a penny the wiser. It is, perhaps, our only hope for Social Credit in England that Parliament may never be called upon to do more than pass it under another name.

IV 4

Until a parliamentary group is formed with a strong backing in the middle and upper classes to bring the Treasury first and the Bank of England afterwards to book, all the manifestoes and resolutions of all the protestant organizations in the country will inevitably be ignored, since they are neither accompanied nor followed by political or any other action. The fact of it is that even the enormity of the Gold superstition is only just beginning to dawn on the present generation, and men still cannot believe that it is as gross and bestial as it is. The tradition of worship still hangs about the Golden Calf. And not even the fact that the price of Gold, or the raw material of the control of Credit, has risen already to more than £6 per ounce and is bound to rise as currencies are depreciated in its interest, will really bring home to men's minds the monstrous simplicity of the Gold and Money Monopoly and its power to control all our lives. From the standpoint of mere commerce, who would not wish to have the commodity in which he deals raised from its natural price of about 15s. an ounce to £6 rising?   III 3

R

We agree, of course, that the present Monopoly is well entrenched both materially and psychologically; it is more, in fact, than an ordinary monopoly, it is an almost universal superstition; and many of its supporters are among its victims. On the other hand, precisely because it is mainly a superstition and not predominantly a brute organization of force, persuasion, with the aid of events, is the most effective weapon to employ against it. The question to be considered, in fact, is not whether persuasion is sufficient, but whether our movement has yet exercised enough of it. Propaganda as a method cannot be said to have failed when it has only been half-hearted and pinched for means; it is the propagandists themselves who have so far failed. Before we abandon our faith in persuasion, we must be convinced that the thousands of adherents of Social Credit are, as a whole, without sincerity, without force of character, without spirit, and incapable, therefore, of persuading even themselves. V 4

Centralized propaganda, besides being contrary to the principles of Social Credit, demands an endowment which no movement of merely universal advantage is ever likely to receive; it will continue, if at all, to be carried on at the personal expense of the unknown few. But the decentralized propaganda that consists in the use by every individual of his own resources to their fullest capacity has all the advantages of effectiveness and none of the disabilities of lack of funds. V 5

Economic power precedes and determines political power; and financial power usually precedes and determines political manœuvres. IV 7

It is useless to plume ourselves on having as yet done more than initiate the discussion of a reform that at the present pace may take several generations to bring into operation. We have obviously scarcely begun to make a dent in the armour of ignorance and prejudice, complacency and selfishness, of the governing classes.   V 10

Given the security of a few more years of peace, we should be content in the confidence of the triumph of Social Credit over all its present critics and enemies. Time is on its side if peace be granted. But as the clouds are indubitably gathering for war on a scale hitherto only dreamed of in nightmare, it appears to be all too probable that civilization may die not only with the cure at its hand but in the presence of doctors who lack only one thing to save their patient—the will.   IV 15

So many sincere reformers manage to get the cart before the horse that it is little wonder that reformers as a body appear to be always at loggerheads and their reforms merely on paper. A Court of Reason, if such existed, to which apparently contending parties could appeal, would be able to eliminate many frictions by the simple device of putting the conflicting proposals in their proper order.

          IV 2

To have stripped away the defences of the secret Money monopoly and to have got down at last to the very nerve is to have made real progress; and we can now, we believe, confidently say that even if this generation should fail to apply itself to the task of mastering the Money power, the coming or some succeeding generation will certainly carry it through. We have our doubts of the competence of this generation for anything but suffering. It would almost appear as if, for the crime of the War, the generation that was responsible for it cannot hate itself enough. With the means to abundant life for all, not only within reach but pressed upon it with all the urgency of modern Science, this generation insists upon fasting and not, like Gandhi, for love of anything, but from hatred of itself. The key to the cupboard of Plenty, however, is exposed at last; and it hangs, as all the world can see, at the entrance to the Central Banks, and its name is Money. Sooner or later, therefore, the world, led by its least sick nation, will recover from its self-abasement and proceed to take the key and open the new age for itself. III 5

In this crisis, we are not exaggerating in saying of human destiny, it is useless, we fear, to depend upon the English people in their present mood of abjection. From top to bottom of society, with comparatively rare exceptions, the individuals of every class appear for the present to be devoid of brains as well as of spirit. Defeatism is practically the general creed of the moment. It is true, of course, that the "emergency" that appears to be necessary to provoke the nation to one of its historic manifestations has not yet presented itself in an obvious form; but it is also true that if the world's intending masters can have their way, it never will. As Mr. Lloyd George has said, the beetles will gnaw at the rafters silently, and the first manifest evidence of their work will be the last. On the other hand, we can take a certain amount of comfort from the fact that even if for the moment we English are sleeping with our backs to the wall, the American people are neither as fast asleep as ourselves nor as disposed to leave their fate to "those in authority". The American people have none of the superstitious reverence with which our people have been carefully taught to regard moneylenders who choose to call themselves "bankers". Again, the American people are too familiar with the open corruption of "legislators" to be in doubt that they are usually secretly corrupt as well. Not only no "experts" are likely to be fully trusted, but, in the last resort, as the world already knows very well, even the promises of its temporary public representatives can be effectively repudiated. It must also be remembered that, in obviousness of emergency, the American people are nearer to the trenches than ourselves. With twelve million destitute unemployed and six million farmers reduced to helotry to the banks, the "emergency" of their national economic situation must strike the American people more forcibly than our own well-cloaked misery. Finally it should be realized in this country that in spite of all the belittling efforts of the bankers and their friends, the *facts* brought to light by "Technocracy" have seized hold upon the imagination of the American people with the power of a vision of the Promised Land, and will now never again be forgotten.

For a situation which, though fundamentally constant, is changing in detail every day, a "Plan"—such, for example, as Major Douglas's Mining Scheme offered in vain to the Miners and Coalowners in 1920—is unsuitable. When Old Age Pensions, Unemployment Insurance or, indeed, any far-reaching piece of proposed social legislation, is under popular discussion the only "Plan" that can be said to exist consists of the objective and a general understanding of the means. The draughting of the Parliamentary Acts themselves is the work of the technical draughtsman and the special Committees. In the same way, when once it is commonly agreed in quarters capable of effective action that the present situation calls urgently for a radical reform in our

Monetary system there need be no doubt in anybody's mind that Plans in plenty will be forthcoming.

Given the will to reorganize our Monetary system in the light of the facts and with the aim of maintaining and consolidating the constitutional and democratic form of social government, the immediate means to this end are relatively simple and could be draughted and made an Act of Parliament in a single session.

The real difficulty in the way of legislating for Social Credit is neither the absence of a Plan nor the absence of popular demand. The difficulty which we confess appears to us for the present to be insuperable is the control now exercised over Parliament itself by the very monopoly which it is essential to any democratic "Plan" to abrogate. If anyone can tell us how to persuade a Parliament largely composed of Bankers' nominees to repudiate its private masters and to legislate for England and not for the Bank of England, we shall listen with respect. But so long as in fact the majority of Members of Parliament, all but one or two members of the Government, and most of the heads of the State services are conscious or unconscious agents of the existing Financial Monopoly, so long, we may be sure, will any "Plan" remain "visionary" and any popular demand ineffective.

II 15

If there is nothing else that President Roosevelt has done, he has at least reasserted the sovereignty of the community over its own Monetary system. By the formal consent cf the Supreme Court, by his own messages to Congress, and with the latter's practically unanimous approval, he has declared the supremacy of the State over the whole of the economic life of the nation, culminating, as it does, in the Monetary system. When it is recalled that he is the first dictator of modern times to realize the priority of financial over every other economic power, and to take full possession of it in the name of the State, it will be realized also how radical, at least potentially, the American experiment may still prove to be. President Roosevelt can say that there is no power in his State greater than the State itself; and that even the Money Monopoly is exercised on suffrance and by the revocable will of the people. How revolutionary this reassertion of a forgotten axiomatic principle of society really is may be measured by the inconceivability of its occurrence in our own country. Though everybody is aware that the Bank of England controls the national Monetary system in the interests of its stockholders, *under a revocable Charter*, everybody is equally aware that no parliament dares even threaten to revoke the Charter, still less to carry the threat into effect. The contempt of the Bank of England for both the Crown and Parliament was revealed in its discarding of even their symbols on its notes; and when a nation and sovereign have consented to their supersession even down to the removal of their symbols it can be taken for granted that their power of resistance to their servant turned master is practically nil. President Roosevelt's courageous reassertion of communal sovereignty over Money is, therefore, at once a hopeful sign for America, and, by contrast, a depressing sign for ourselves.   IV 15

So long as the middle and upper classes, as a whole, remain unconvinced or unpersuaded of the desirability, even and especially from their own point of view, of a radical change in our economic system, so long, we believe, will any radical change be impracticable. It is patent, furthermore, to many of us that the resources of revolution by constitution are not only not exhausted, but the Labour party in Parliament has never begun to use them. If, as we believe, a radical change in our Monetary system is desirable in the interests of the whole nation, rentier, wage-earner, professional and salariat equally, it is bad policy, to say the least of it, to demand the change in the interests of one class alone, and, above all, of a class which, in point of fact, machinery is daily making more and more superfluous. It is probably impossible, given the mentality of the existing Parliamentary Labour group, to expect of it a change of objective or even of tactics.

II 1

Accepting it as axiomatic that, in fact, the economic system of any nation is under the control of its Central Bank, and the patent fact that the economic system has broken down, the obviously responsible parties for both its breakdown and its repair are the Central Banks themselves. And if, as appears to be the case, the Central Banks deny responsibility while still continuing to exercise the sovereign power of veto, there would seem to be no alternatives before a desperately suffering and imminently doomed nation but to force its Monetary Monopolists either to get on with the national job or to get out.

I 20

Until, in fact, the present personnel at both the Treasury and the Bank of England is scrapped and superseded, it is practically impossible for any reform in our Monetary system to be effected. In an article published in 1933 in the *Daily Herald*, Major Douglas suggested as the only means by which the ordinary citizen can affect a change of policy is that everybody should bombard his Member of Parliament with appeals and complaints. But without deprecating any form of action that is not subversive, it does not appear to us or, we imagine, to Major Douglas himself, that appeals by post to Members of Parliament who themselves, by all the signs, share the *idées fixes* of the Financial hierarchy are likely to be of much avail. Apart from the slow and by no means sure process of public education in matters of Finance (and we, if anybody, should know how slow, uncertain and ungrateful a task it is), we can depend, it appears to us, upon only two factors: the inevitability of the progressive break-up of Society with its alarming periods of crisis, and, in the last resort, the awakening of conscience and resolution in the depths of the English character. That the present Depression will not pass, like its predecessors, as a result of a lucky chance, we are convinced. The pitcher is broken at the well this time. The doubtful question that the next few years must answer is whether there remains a string to the English bow.   II 21

We must confess that if our diagnosis is incorrect and, in spite of all the symptoms to the contrary, the Bank of England and the Treasury should prove to be right in their belief that the Depression will pass, and International Trade be restored, then not only is our diagnosis discredited, but the prescription of Social Credit must expect to be regarded as a counsel of perfection. For we are under no illusion that in the absence of stark necessity Social Credit is likely to be adopted by any nation voluntarily and as a measure of reason and justice. Motives of this high order appeal to individuals but not to nations. The question, however, is: At what stage the Depression, if it continues, will be accepted as chronic; and, again: At what stage of the decline of international Investment will it be practically concluded that Economic Nationalism is here to stay? For many diseases, if they are recognized for what they are in time, there is a remedy; and, likewise, for many symptoms of healthy growth, if they are recognized in time, there are favourable adaptations to be made. But just as both diseases and growth may fail to be recognized in time for their proper treatment, there is the no small danger that only when it is too late will the Depression be accepted as chronic and the rise of Economic Nationalism as a symptom of healthy growth. Nations before us, civilizations before us, have died from failure to read the signs of their times. Spain and Holland died as Powers from failure to realize the vital importance of discovering an alternative to the Gold Standard. The Roman Empire fell at the end of a prolonged period of Depression which none of its Governments had the courage to declare chronic or the intelligence to treat. The present Depression among ourselves has already (1934) lasted some sixteen years, during which, save for occasional blood-transfusions, the state of International Investment has likewise been going from bad to worse. We ask ourselves again: When will the disease be admitted and hope of natural recovery be abandoned for rational treatment? How many years must the symptoms be recorded before a fresh diagnosis is made? Or must the symptoms be fatal before they even succeed in being alarming?   V 26

The impression must be corrected, if possible, that we are "anti-bankers". In the first place it is humanely impossible to sustain an attitude of enmity to men who appealingly declare that all that bankers do is to safeguard their depositors' money. Enmity is dissolved into pity in face of innocence such as this. In the second place, it is not only true that, in our own country at least, the administration of the banks is almost beyond criticism; we rely upon it, in fact, as both the working model of future financial administration and the answer to the objection that monetary administration is bound to become either inefficient or corrupt; but it is also true that under a system of Social Credit there will be greater rather than less use for banks and bankers than there is at present. The administration of a National Credit Account easily a hundred times greater than the present restricted Monopoly Credit Account will certainly entail both an extension of banking personnel and the multiplication of branches. No banker or banking employee is therefore likely to lose his job under Social Credit unless, as it still occasionally occurs, it is already a sinecure. Finally it is manifestly true that without the goodwill of the present banking-staffs it will be difficult if not impossible to inaugurate Social Credit without risk of failure. Our peaceful transition, in short, from an out-of-date to a modern Monetary system, presupposes the co-operation of the present administrators with at least goodwill if not with complete understanding. The indictment, on the other hand, of the Banking system itself is as severe as the approval of its personnel is unaffectedly friendly. To begin with, it is one of the worst of things, a Monopoly; and one of the worst of Monopolies, the monopoly of an absolutely universal necessity. Acting as a Monopoly, moreover, it is under the maximum degree of temptation to sustain and fortify itself as such if only to ensure its own existence. All the rules of so-called "Sound Finance", in fact, are rules adopted by the Monopoly for its own preservation. Though the monopoly consists of Money, a factor unique in society, the ordinary rules of Monopoly are applied to it: the price of Money is maintained by manipulating supply. And, since the monopoly itself is one of use and not one of possession, the Money in question is never absolutely parted with but only lent; in other words, even the limited amount of Money permitted to Society begins and remains as somebody's debt to the banking system. V 5

If it is constantly kept in mind that the vital monetary issue today is: Who shall control the National Credit?— the apparently slow pace of change will be better understood. The principle of royal personal absolutism was not superseded by constitutional monarchism in a mere decade and it is practically certain that the transition from the absolute and personal principle of Money Control, now vested in the stockholders of the private Central Banks of every country, will not be universally made without a series and a period of struggles. IV 16

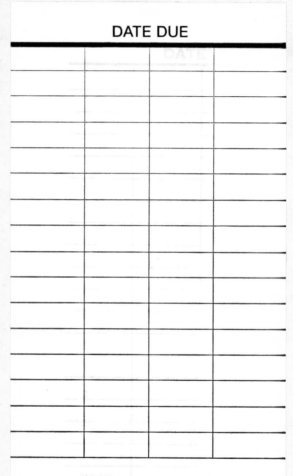

DATE DUE